General editor

Peter Herriot

New Essential Psychology

Experimental Design and Statistics

ALREADY PUBLISHED IN THIS SERIES

Applying Psychology in Organizations
Frank Blackler and Sylvia Shimmin

Cognitive Development and Education
Johanna Turner

Individual Differences
Theories and applications
V.J. Shackleton and C.A. Fletcher

Instinct, Environment and Behaviour
S.E.G. Lea

Learning Theory and Behaviour Modification
Stephen Walker

Lifespan Development
Concepts, theories and interventions
Léonie Sugarman

Personality Theory and Clinical Practice
Peter Fonagy and Anna Higgitt

Selves in Relation
Keith Oatley

Social Interaction and its Management
Judy Gahagan

FORTHCOMING TITLES IN THE SERIES

Attitudes and Decisions
J. Richard Eiser and Joop van der Pligt

Human Physiological Psychology
Theory and applications
Tony Gale

Information and Human Performance
Paul J. Barber and David Legge

Memory, Thinking and Language
Topics in cognitive psychology
Judith Greene

Multivariate Design and Statistics
Steve Miller

Steve Miller

Experimental Design and Statistics

SECOND EDITION

Routledge

London and New York

First published in 1974 by
Methuen & Co. Ltd

Second edition 1984
Reprinted 1986

Reprinted 1989, 1991
by Routledge
11 New Fetter Lane, London EC4P 4EE
29 West 35th Street, New York, NY 10001

Typeset by Cotswold Typesetting Ltd
Printed in Great Britain by
Richard Clay (The Chaucer Press) Ltd
Bungay, Suffolk

British Library Cataloguing in Publication Data

Miller, Steve, 1943–
Experimental design and statistics—2nd ed. (New essential psychology)
I. *Psychology*
I. Title II. Series
150 BF121

Library of Congress Cataloging in Publication Data
Miller, Stephen H. (Stephen Henry), 1943–
Experimental design and statistics. (New essential psychology)
Bibliography: p.
Includes index
1. Psychology, Experimental. 2. Experimental design. 3. Psychometrics. I. Title. II. Series
BF191.M54
1984 150'.724 83–23833

ISBN 0-415-04011-6

Contents

Table of statistical tests included in this book

TYPE OF DATA	TYPE OF RESEARCH DESIGN					
	One-sample	*Two-sample*		*k sample*		*Correlation*
		Related	Independent	Related	Independent	
Parametric tests	One-sample Z (p. 114) One-sample t (p. 117)	Related t-test (p. 100)	Independent Z-test (p. 79) Independent t-test (p. 82) Variance ratio (F)-test			Product–moment correlation coefficient (Pearson r) (p. 135) Linear regression (p. 147)
Non-parametric tests	One-sample proportions test (p. 120)	Wilcoxon test (p. 104) Sign test (p. 107)	Mann-Whitney test (p. 86) χ^2 test (2×2) (p. 90)	Page's L trend test (p. 128)	Jonckheere trend test (p. 126)	Spearman's rank correlation coefficient (p. 140)

1

Designing an experiment

The scientific approach to behaviour

Psychologists do not have an exclusive claim on the study of human behaviour. Many philosophers, writers, poets, theologians, and even salesmen are interested in the nature of human thought and action. And indeed, there is a sense in which we all possess some sort of personal 'theory' of behaviour, a theory which is used to guide our relationships with other people and to help us predict each other's reactions and sensitivities.

Now each of these different approaches can sometimes produce perfectly respectable psychological theories. For example, the popular belief, 'Once bitten, twice shy', has its counterpart in the psychological literature on punishment. And some theological views, such as the belief that suffering induces more tolerant attitudes, could easily be the starting-point for a programme of psychological research. So we cannot claim that there is a basic difference between the theories put forward by psychologists and those devised by other students and observers of human nature. The distinguishing feature of experimental psychology is not so much the nature of its theories as the *methods used to test their validity*. The approach adopted is essentially *scientific*; a psychological theory has to fit the facts of behaviour as derived from systematic observations taken in carefully controlled conditions. If a theory does not fit the facts it is discarded or revised, no matter how long its history, how appealing its logic, or how convenient its implications. As we shall see, this emphasis on objectivity and rigorous control narrows the range of behaviour that can feasibly be studied, but in return it produces more solid and reliable conclusions.

Thus we have defined experimental psychology mainly in terms of its *methodology*, i.e. the procedures used to evaluate theories. But we have placed no limits on the way in which these theories are first devised. They may be based on years of exploratory research, on a vague hunch, or even on a political or religious viewpoint. It doesn't really matter so long as the theories give rise to *predictions* which can be tested against the behaviour of human beings in controlled settings. This is the basis of scientific psychology.

Predictions in psychology

What does a prediction from a psychological theory actually look like? Here are some examples:

1 Highly aroused subjects respond more rapidly to visual stimuli than sleepy subjects.
2 Reaction time to sounds is faster than reaction time to visual stimuli.
3 Daydreaming occurs more frequently during simple tasks than complex tasks.
4 The amount of saliva produced by a dog when a bell is rung depends on how frequently the sound of the bell was previously associated with feeding.
5 Two letters can be classified as having the same *name* more rapidly if they are identical (e.g. AA) than if they differ in case (e.g. Aa).
6 Driving skill varies as a function of the level of alcohol in the blood.

These predictions (or *experimental hypotheses*) differ in a number of ways. Some accord very much with common sense whereas others do not. Some are based on rather complex theoretical notions whereas others seem to reflect a very simple model of behaviour. Some are clearly related to everyday behaviour whereas others deal with seemingly obscure psychological tasks. What is common to them all, however, is their general format. In effect each prediction is saying that as one thing changes there will be consequential change in something else: as arousal increases response time decreases, as task complexity increases so frequency of daydreaming decreases, as alcohol level changes so driving skill changes, and so on. Each of the above predictions has the same basic logical form although the sentence structure varies slightly from one case to another.

A prediction, then, is a statement that a change in one thing (the *independent variable* or IV) will produce a change in another thing (the *dependent variable* or DV). Thus a change in arousal level (the IV) is said to produce a change in response time (the DV). Task complexity (the IV) influences frequency of daydreaming (the DV). And variations in alcohol level (the IV) cause changes in driving skill (the DV). In general the independent variable will relate to a change in the *conditions* governing behaviour and the dependent variable will correspond to some measure of the subject's behaviour or *performance* under those conditions.

Testing a prediction: the role of experimental design and statistics

How do we go about testing a psychological prediction? Clearly we need some sort of plan for collecting information or *data* about the relationship between the independent and dependent variables. The formulation of a plan for collecting relevant data is known as *research design.*

Consider, for example, the prediction that driving skill is affected by the level of blood alcohol. One possible plan for data collection would be to ask a sample of drivers whether they had experienced any change in their driving skill after drinking. This wouldn't be a very good research design for obvious reasons. Drivers are probably very poor at estimating changes in their own skill even when they are sober. But we would be asking them to *remember* changes which took place while in various states of intoxication. Even if they could recall such information it is doubtful whether they would willingly report their own reckless or anti-social behaviour just because we asked them. So this approach would lead to unreliable and possibly biased results.

An alternative plan would be to collect our data from various official records of accident rates. We would be interested, for example, in the proportion of accidents involving drunken drivers. We could also compare accident rates before and after the introduction of stricter legislation on drink and driving. Or we could look at changes in accident rates as a function of the times at which public houses are open for the sale of drinks. Data of this kind would lead to rather tentative conclusions about the effects of alcohol level on driving skill. Although this sort of evidence is reasonably objective, it is none the less circumstantial.

Scientists are generally agreed that the most effective means of testing a prediction is deliberately to manipulate the independent variable and then to observe the consequential changes in the dependent variable. It is only this method of collecting data – the *experimental* method – which has the power to reveal cause-and-effect relationships in an unambiguous way. Thus the best way of testing whether alcohol influences driving skill is to actually administer different quantities of alcohol to groups of volunteers and to compare their performance in a subsequent driving task. This direct, experimental approach will produce more definite results than the methods based on the observation of *natural* events, such as a survey of accident rates in relation to the availability of drinks.

We are committed in this book to the use of experimental methods in testing psychological predictions. In this first chapter we shall discuss the different ways in which data can be collected in an experiment – this is the topic of *experimental design*. Our main interest is to decide how subjects should be divided between the various conditions of the experiment. Such questions of layout should not be decided arbitrarily. The idea of experimental design is to ensure that the data emerging at the end of an experiment are relevant to the prediction being tested and not contaminated by outside factors. In other words, an experiment has to be designed in such a way that its results will logically confirm or refute the predicted effects of the independent variable. It is surprisingly easy to sabotage these aims by carelessness at the design stage of an experiment.

Let us assume, for the moment, that an experiment has been adequately designed and carried out. The next step is to interpret the results to see if they support our prediction. Now it rarely happens – even with the best laid designs – that the results are completely clear cut. One would be pleasantly surprised if *all* the subjects in one condition produced dramatically different behaviour from *all* the subjects in another condition. We normally get some overlap between the performance of the two groups, some blurring of the effects of the independent variable. This is where *statistics* come in – to tell us whether we can draw any general conclusions from the data, or whether there is too much blur to say anything. We shall return to this problem and the various techniques needed to solve it in the coming chapters. But before we do this we must establish the basic logic of an experiment and the principles underlying its design.

What exactly is an experiment?

In formal terms an experiment is a means of collecting evidence to show the effect of one variable upon another. In the ideal case the experimenter manipulates the IV, holds *all* other variables constant, and then observes the changes in the DV. In this hypothetical, perfect experiment any changes in the DV must be caused by the manipulation of the IV.

Suppose, for example, we have a theory which predicts that sleep deprivation causes an increase in reaction time to visual signals. Given the co-operation of a group of subjects we could test this prediction experimentally. Half the subjects would be deprived of sleep for one night while the remaining half were allowed to sleep normally. The next morning we would measure the reaction time of each subject and see whether the sleep deprived group had noticeably longer reaction times. If they had, and provided that the two groups were similar in all other respects, we would be justified in concluding that sleep deprivation causes a slowing of reactions to visual stimuli. This procedure qualifies as an experiment because we have actually *manipulated* the independent variable (amount of sleep) and observed the consequential changes in the dependent variable (reaction time). This is the simplest type of experiment – one in which the independent variable takes on only *two* values or *levels* (no sleep – normal sleep). We shall focus on this basic design for most of the book, but the principles will apply equally to more complex experiments in which we compare the effects of *three* or more levels of the independent variable (e.g. no sleep – two hours' sleep – normal sleep).

Now let us consider a second example. This time we have a theory which predicts a relationship between, say, intelligence and reaction time: intelligent subjects are expected to react faster than less intelligent subjects. Again we might divide our group of willing volunteers into two sub-groups, this time according to their IQs. Thus we would form a more intelligent group and a less intelligent group. If we found the predicted difference in reaction times we might be tempted to conclude that intelligence determines the speed of a subject's reactions, just as sleep deprivation did in the previous example. The analogy is misleading, however, because intelligence cannot be deliberately manipulated in the way that sleep deprivation can. Subjects bring their own level of intelligence with them to the laboratory, and all we can do is to *observe* the relationship between intelligence and reaction time. But we cannot go on to infer a cause-and-effect relationship between the two variables because both of them may be influenced by a third, uncontrolled variable. For example, it may be that intelligent subjects tend to be healthier than less intelligent subjects, or younger, or more highly motivated, or more attentive . . .; any one of a number of such variables might be the real *cause* of the variation in reaction time. We might be mistaken if we ascribed the causal role to intelligence rather than one of the other variables which happens to be related to intelligence. This example highlights the major weakness of all non-experimental research; we can never be certain whether the independent variable we measure is actually the one that produces changes in the dependent variable.

Unfortunately many of the variables we would like to investigate cannot be brought under experimental control. We cannot manipulate a subject's personal characteristics: his age, sex, social status, intelligence, personality, religious beliefs, social attitudes, and so on. Nor would we want to interfere with critical aspects of a subject's physiological or emotional state, even though this might be possible in principle. In such cases the researcher has to fall back on observing natural variations in the variables of interest. He compares the performance of old and young subjects, or males and females, or, as in the above example, more and less intelligent subjects. He then has to resort to statistical procedures to rule out the possible influences of uncontrolled factors which may be changing together with the variable under study. The procedures which are used in this type of study are discussed in more detail in other texts under the heading of *correlational designs* (see, for example, Chatfield and Collins, 1980; Miller, forthcoming). They are of critical importance in such subjects as social psychology, sociology and economics where experimental control of the independent variables is usually impossible or unrealistic. But the experimental psychologist can avoid the complications of correlational studies if he is prepared to limit his research to variables which can be manipulated experimentally. This means, in effect, that he is going to be more concerned with the influence of external conditions on performance than with the effect of the characteristics of his subjects. It also means he will be less plagued by the problems of psychological measurement. The *manipulation* of independent variables like the brightness of a stimulus or the length of a word is much more straightforward than the *measurement* of independent variables like intelligence or neuroticism.

Irrelevant variables

So far the reader may have gained the impression that there are no unwanted variables in an experiment – that all the variation in the subjects' performance will be caused by changes in the independent variable. This might be true of a scientific paradise, but in the real world it is impossible to hold constant all those variables which might influence the subjects' behaviour in an experiment. Take, for example, our investigation of the effects of sleep deprivation on reaction time. How could we ensure that all our subjects are equally attentive and well motivated, or that they have equally acute vision? Can we be certain that the apparatus will remain equally sensitive throughout the experiment, or that the background noises and distractions will be the same for each subject? And how can we eliminate any changes in the experimenter's tone of voice or general attitude to the subjects? Even changes in the room temperature or time of day might affect a subject's reaction time. There are a large number of variables that might, in principle, affect the dependent variable, although we are only interested in the effects of sleep deprivation. For the purposes of our experiment, then, all the other factors may be thought of as *irrelevant variables.*

The effect of irrelevant variables

It would be useful if we could hold all of these irrelevant variables constant and just manipulate the independent variable. Then we would get a perfectly clear picture of its effect on the subject's behaviour. But such complete control over all irrelevant variables can never be achieved. It is either physically impossible (e.g. how can one hold the sensitivity of the apparatus constant?) or practically inconvenient (e.g. imagine trying to hold noise, temperature, humidity and illumination constant). And in any case there are reasons why too much control is actually undesirable (see p. 156). So we have to resign ourselves to the presence of some irrelevant variables in every experiment we undertake. The question is whether such variables could undermine the logic of the experiment itself.

The only way in which this could happen is for an irrelevant variable to change its value *systematically* across the two conditions of the experiment. We then have the independent variable and the irrelevant variable changing together, so that any difference between the scores obtained in the two conditions becomes impossible to interpret; it could be caused by the irrelevant variable, or the independent variable, or the combined effects of both. Suppose, for example, that our subjects in the sleep deprivation experiment have to be tested in two rooms, one of which is warmer than the other. Room temperature then becomes an irrelevant variable which might influence a subject's reaction time. If, for some reason, we tested all the sleep deprived subjects in the warmer room and all the non-deprived subjects in the cooler room, then we would not know how to interpret a difference between the performance of the two groups. If our results show that the sleep deprived group have, say, longer reaction times than the non-deprived group, we are unable to say whether lack of sleep or the warm environment were responsible. The point is that we can never disentangle the effects of two variables that change together.

The irrelevant variable in such cases is known as a *confounding factor* because it literally confounds our interpretation of the experiment.

Of course confounding doesn't just happen, it is of our own making – and it can usually be avoided. Thus in the previous example we could decide randomly for each subject which room was to be used. This wouldn't remove the effect of the irrelevant variable altogether – changes in room temperature would still be causing variations in reaction time – but the effects would be spread more or less evenly across the two experimental conditions. This then is the second way in which irrelevant variables can influence the results of an experiment – by varying randomly from subject to subject but *not* tending to influence one condition any more or less than another. Non-systematic effects of this kind are called *random* effects, and they do not undermine the logic of an experiment. However, they do tend to *obscure* the effects of the independent variable because they increase the variability in each set of scores. Thus when we come to compare the two sets we do not see the effects of the independent variable so clearly (see table 1).

Table 1 Imaginary results of the sleep deprivation experiment (*a*) with and (*b*) without random effects

(a) Reaction time to visual stimuli in milliseconds		*(b) Reaction time to visual stimuli in milliseconds*	
Sleep deprived (5 subjects)	*Normal sleep (5 subjects)*	*Sleep deprived (5 subjects)*	*Normal sleep (5 subjects)*
450	420	450	420
470	450	450	420
430	400	450	420
420	440	450	420
480	390	450	420
Average 450	420	450	420

Methods of controlling irrelevant variables

The major purpose of *experimental control* is to avoid

confounding – that is, to ensure that the *only* variable which changes systematically from one condition to another is the independent variable. Without this our experiment becomes uninterpretable. The second aim is to minimize the random variation in the data so as to highlight the effect of the independent variable. With these aims in mind we shall now introduce the various methods of control

A preliminary point: we need to distinguish between those irrelevant variables associated with the subject – intelligence, motivation, personality, etc. – and those associated with the conditions under which the experiment is conducted – background noise, instructions, experimenter's tone of voice, etc. We shall call the former *subject variables* and the latter *situational variables.* Although both classes of irrelevant variable may threaten our experiment in the same way, they are controlled in different ways.

The control of subject variables

In controlling subject variables we want to ensure that the groups of subjects tested under each experimental condition are as similar as possible on all the dimensions along which people can differ. We do this by carefully controlling *the way in which subjects are allocated to the experimental conditions.* There are three possible methods:

(1) THE REPEATED MEASURES DESIGN

The only way we can be sure that our two groups of subjects will have identical characteristics is to use the *same* subjects in each group. This is what we do in a *repeated measures* design; each subject performs under *both* conditions of the experiment so that the effects of subject variables will balance out exactly. This is the most effective method of control. By analysing the difference between the two scores belonging to each subject we obtain a very sensitive measure of the effects of the independent variable, a measure which is uncontaminated by any variations in subject characteristics.

Suppose, for example, we were investigating the effect of word length on the ease of remembering a list of ten words. Using a repeated measures design our group of subjects would be tested

Table 2 The layout of a repeated measures design

Independent variable	
Level I (e.g. long words)	*Level II (e.g. short words)*
S_1	S_1
S_2	S_2
S_3	S_3
S_4	S_4
.	.
.	.
.	.

Note: S_1, S_2, S_3, stand for different subjects.

for their memory of a list of short words, and the *same* group would be tested on a list of long words (see table 2). This arrangement would give us perfect control over troublesome variables like differences in the subjects' learning abilities, or levels of motivation which might otherwise contaminate the results. But, in return, we now have to cope with a new irrelevant variable, i.e. whether a task is performed first or second. The task that is performed second may benefit from practice acquired in the first, or may, perhaps, suffer from the effects of fatigue or boredom. *Order effects* of this kind can easily lead to confounding. Thus if all our subjects perform the two tasks in the same order, any differences that emerge could be caused either by the change in word length, or by a change in fatigue, practice, or whatever. We must therefore ensure that the order in which the tasks are performed is *counterbalanced* across subjects – that is, half the subjects follow one order, and the other half follow the reverse order. Alternatively, we could decide on the order randomly for each subject, say by tossing a coin. Normally such steps will ensure that the order effects will balance out over the experiment as a whole, but there is no guarantee of this. If the order effects are *asymmetrical*, e.g. one task produces *greater* fatigue than the other, then we cannot expect the order effects to be neutralized by counterbalancing, or any similar device. Thus the repeated measures design should only be used when we judge the order effects to be symmetrical or insignificant. For a critical discussion of this point, see Poulton (1980).

(2) THE MATCHED SUBJECTS DESIGN

Sometimes it is possible to 'imitate' the repeated measures design without actually using the same subjects in each condition. This can be done when we have pairs of very similar individuals (e.g. identical twins), or where we can select pairs who are *very similar on the variables that influence the behaviour under study*. Suppose, for example, we were conducting an experiment to compare the effects of two different types of instructions on the speed with which a problem is solved. It would be nice if we could equate the two conditions on subject variables by using a repeated measures design. But since we cannot test a subject twice on the *same* problem, this design is inappropriate. The next best thing is to use a matched subjects design (see table 3) in which each pair of subjects is matched on, say, intelligence and creativity. We would then allocate one member of each pair to the first condition, and the other

Table 3 The layout of a matched subjects design

	Independent variable	
	Level I	*Level II*
Pair 1	S_{1a}	S_{1b}
Pair 2	S_{2a}	S_{2b}
Pair 3	S_{3a}	S_{3b}
Pair 4	S_{4a}	S_{4b}
.	.	.
.	.	.
.	.	.

Note: S_{1a} stands for the subject in pair 1 who was allocated to level I of the experiment; S_{1b} stands for the subject allocated to level II. Similarly for other pairs of subjects.

member to the second condition – the allocation being made on a random basis. The difference between each pair of scores would then reflect the influence of type of instructions, and would be largely free of subject effects. But note that this would only be true if the subjects were matched on the right variables, i.e. those that have a large effect on problem solving behaviour. If we match subjects on variables that are unrelated to the dependent variable this design becomes extremely insensitive.

A major drawback of the matched subjects design is the difficulty of knowing which subject variables should form the basis of the matching. And even if we can identify the most influential variables, it is often a difficult and time consuming matter to actually recruit pairs of subjects whose scores on these variables are closely matched. Consequently this design is not met very frequently outside the literature on twin studies.

(3) INDEPENDENT GROUPS DESIGN

It should be clear by now that rigorous control over subject variables cannot always be achieved. Often we have to fall back on a third method of control – the *independent groups* design (table 4) – which is less sensitive to the effects of the independent variable, but can be used freely for almost any experiment.

In this design subjects are divided into two entirely separate groups on the basis of a strictly random procedure. This could

Table 4 The layout of an independent groups design

Independent variable	
Level I	*Level II*
S_1	S_2
S_3	S_4
S_5	S_6
S_7	S_8
.	.
.	.
.	.

Note: S_1, S_2, S_3, etc. stand for different subjects.

be done by asking each subject to draw a number from a hat, there being as many numbers as subjects. The subjects who draw even numbers are then assigned to one condition, and those who draw odd numbers to the other condition. An obviously non-random technique would be to place all the female subjects in one condition and all the male subjects in the other. Not quite so obvious, but equally non-random, is the procedure of allocating the front rows of a room full of subjects to one condition, and the back rows to the other condition. There could easily be a systematic difference, say in personality, between subjects who gravitate to the front of a room and those who sit at the back.

Provided that the subjects are randomly allocated to the two conditions we would expect the groups to be fairly well matched on the subject variables. That is, they should have about the same overall levels of intelligence, attentiveness, creativity, etc. Note that randomization doesn't ensure that the two groups will be *perfectly* matched on any particular subject variable. All we can say is that there will be no *systematic* bias in favour of one group. In the long run, if we were to continue the random allocation indefinitely, all the differences would balance out. But given the small numbers of subjects typically available in psychology experiments we cannot expect this to happen. We therefore have to try to decide whether the difference between our two groups of scores is due to the independent variable or simply to the irrelevant variables that did not quite balance out in the randomization process. The greater the variation caused by the subject variables, the more difficult this decision becomes.

Unlike the previous designs, the independent groups design does not allow us to remove the effects of subject variables from the background random variation. Hence this design is rather insensitive. Using more advanced techniques it is possible to improve on the basic independent groups design, but these techniques are beyond the scope of this book (see Myers, 1962, ch. 12). One improvement that can be made, however, is to remove the random effects of some subject variables by holding them *constant*. Thus if we felt that variations in our subjects' visual acuity might 'swamp' the effects of the independent variable in a visual perception experiment, we could improve the sensitivity of our design by restricting the study to subjects whose visual acuity fell between some specified limits. In this way fluctuations in visual acuity would not contribute to the random variation in the data.

THE CONTROL OF SUBJECT VARIABLES – A SUMMARY

The three methods of control may now be ranked in the following order from most effective to least effective:

1 Repeated measures
2 Matched subjects
3 Independent groups

All three methods eliminate *systematic* differences between the conditions of an experiment as far as subject characteristics are concerned. But they differ in the amount of random variation which remains to obscure the experimental effect. The repeated measures design allows us to remove *all* the random variation between subjects; the matched subjects design eliminates some, but not all, of this random variation; and the independent groups design eliminates none at all (although by selecting subjects with a uniform rating on certain variables we can remove the random variation they would have produced).

Although our order of preference between these techniques is now clear, the actual choice will consist of finding the best method appropriate to the particular study. We have summarized how this choice can be made in figure 1.

The control of situational variables

Variations in the characteristics of our subjects are not the only factors that may jeopardize an experiment. We also need to control the variables associated with the experimental situation itself – background noise, apparatus changes, the experimenter's behaviour, and so forth. Such factors could easily confound the effects of the independent variable if they changed systematically from one condition to another. The most effective way of avoiding this is to hold the variables in question *constant* throughout the experiment. Thus we could remove variations in background noise by conducting the experiment in a sound-proof cubicle. Clearly once we have held such variables constant they cannot interfere in any way with the effects of the independent variable. But the effort involved in holding situational variables constant tends to make us

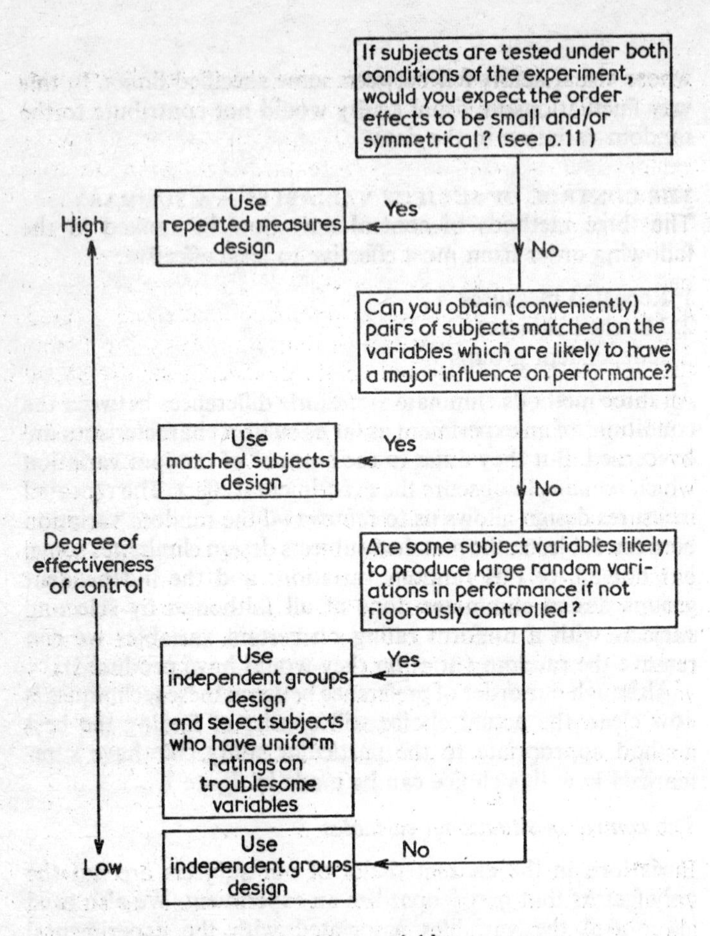

Figure 1 How to control subject variables

reluctant to use it, except for variables which are likely to produce large fluctuations in performance. For example, we would probably hold background noise constant in an experiment on the perception of weak sounds, but we might not consider it worthwhile in a memory experiment or a study of problem solving.

Apart from the effort involved, there will be some variables that simply cannot be held constant. For example, it may be necessary to test subjects on different days of the week, or to use several experimenters during the course of the study. We may even change some variables intentionally, say the vehicles used in a driving experiment, in order to give the findings more general applicability. The way to deal with such variables is to *balance* their effects across the two conditions of the experiment. Thus if two experimenters were used we would make sure that half the subjects in each group were tested by each experimenter. This procedure removes the 'experimenter' variable as a source of *bias*, but its effects are not completely eliminated. The important point, however, is that variables controlled in this way cannot produce systematic changes in the dependent variable.

There is a limit to the number of factors that can be controlled by these more rigorous methods. In a typical experiment it would only be feasible to control a small proportion of situational variables by balancing or by holding them constant. Hence we need a technique for 'mopping up' all the situational variables that we are unwilling or unable to control in other ways. This technique is *randomization*. In the case of situational variables this means testing our subjects in a *random order* rather than dealing with each condition in turn. In this way any variables that might change systematically through time, such as the experimenter's temper or the functioning of the apparatus, will affect the two conditions about equally.

Other aspects of experimental design

In this chapter we have discussed the control of irrelevant variables in some detail, and yet we have said next to nothing about certain other features of the experiment. For example, how do we select subjects for an experiment? How many subjects should be tested under each condition? Can we compare several levels of the independent variable, or must it always be two? And what about the dependent variable? Are some ways of measuring behaviour more suitable than others? Such questions need to be answered, and will be in the remaining chapters (particularly chapter 10). But we have singled out the question of experimental control because this is *fundamental* to the very logic of an experiment. The success of the whole exercise depends on our ability to treat both conditions alike in all respects other than the independent variable.

Chapter summary

1 Experimental psychology is concerned with the objective testing of predictions about behaviour using experimental methods.
2 A prediction is a statement that a change in certain conditions (the independent variable) will produce a change in some aspect of a person's behaviour (the dependent variable).
3 The most effective method of testing a prediction is to *manipulate* the independent variable, hold all other variables constant, and observe the changes in the dependent variable. This constitutes an *experiment.*
4 When conducting an experiment there are very many variables that could influence behaviour apart from the independent variable. These other variables are known as *irrelevant* variables, and can be subdivided into *subject* variables (e.g. intelligence, personality characteristics, etc.) and *situational* variables (e.g. background noise, experimenter's tone of voice, etc.).
5 It is impossible to hold all irrelevant variables constant throughout an experiment. But it is essential that no variable is allowed to change *systematically* with the independent variable. When this happens the experiment is said to be *confounded,* i.e. we cannot disentangle the effects of the independent variable and the irrelevant variable that changes with it.
6 The purposes of experimental control are (1) to eliminate any risk of confounding, and (2) to minimize the random effects of irrelevant variables.
7 In the case of subject variables these aims are achieved by carefully controlling the way in which subjects are allocated to the experimental conditions. The three basic designs, in order of effectiveness, are: (1) repeated measures, (2) matched subjects and (3) independent groups (least effective).
8 Situational variables may be physically held *constant* through the experiment, *balanced* across the two conditions, or allowed to vary *randomly* from subject to subject. We can ensure random variation by testing subjects from the two groups in random order.

comparing the effects of hot and cold environments, for example, neither treatment could be considered more 'basic' than the other, so that the experimental/control distinction would be inappropriate. Instead we would refer simply to the 'hot' and 'cold' conditions.

Having defined the conditions of an experiment we must decide on the general layout – that is, the manner in which subjects will be allocated to the two conditions. From the point of view of controlling subject variables a repeated measures design would be preferable (see pp. 10–12). But since a logical reasoning test cannot be employed twice on the same subjects – at least not if the second assessment is to be meaningful – this option must be rejected. Let us also suppose that we do not have the time to set about finding subjects who can be matched on appropriate variables like intelligence and perseverance. This rules out the matched subjects design, and leaves us with the independent groups design in which subjects are randomly divided into two groups – one for each condition of the experiment. This design is clearly appropriate, although it is rather insensitive to the effects of the independent variable. We can improve matters a little, however, by restricting our experiment to, say, mathematics students at a particular university. This will considerably reduce the amount of random variation in the data because individual differences in logical reasoning ability will be quite small. Hopefully, then, the effects of traffic noise on performance will not be masked by large random fluctuations between subjects' scores.

We have now outlined the basic design of the experiment – two independent groups of subjects will be used, with say, twenty people in each group. Subjects in the experimental group will be required to complete a logical reasoning test while traffic noise can be heard. The control group will perform the same task but will not be exposed to the traffic noise. The difference between the performance of the two groups will provide the evidence required to test our prediction.

Now this basic design is all very well, but it does not enable us to go away and actually run an experiment. We have to decide on a large number of *procedural* matters first. For example, how, exactly, are we going to manipulate traffic noise? What test will be used to measure logical reasoning, and how will it be scored? Precisely what instructions will be given to the subjects? Will they have a time limit, and if so will they be kept informed of the time they have left? In what type of surroundings will the subjects be tested?

(3) Answering these questions is equivalent to translating the basic experimental design into a concrete specification of exactly what has to be done to run the experiment. We shall refer to this as *operationalizing* the experiment. Many of these operational details will appear trivial, for example, specifying the features of the experimental room, but other aspects make us think more precisely about exactly what it is we are trying to discover. For example, the question of how we are going to manipulate traffic noise makes us think about the inferences we wish to draw from the experiment. Are we interested in showing that unusually high levels of noise can impair mental performance relative to near silence? Or are we more interested in the effects of a 'typically' noisy environment (say an office adjacent to a major road) compared with a quiet, but realistic, work environment (say an office in a side road with good sound insulation)? Both of these questions are perfectly legitimate, although the second is obviously more relevant to practical problems of noise control. Assuming we chose the second approach we would probably go out and make tape recordings of background noise in the two types of environment, and use these recordings to define the two conditions of the experiment.

Turning now to the dependent variable, we should ask ourselves precisely how we expect performance to be impaired. Are we anticipating that noise will gradually wear our subjects down during the course of the task, or do we expect a fairly constant level of impairment throughout the task? Is traffic noise likely to induce an increase in errors on the reasoning test, or a slowing of performance, or some of both? Perhaps our theoretical ideas about the effects of noise are not advanced enough to allow us to make such specific predictions. In this case we might decide to measure performance in a general way – say the number of correct solutions achieved in thirty minutes on a particular logical reasoning test. We could analyse the effects more thoroughly in a later experiment.

As a final example of procedural detail we shall consider the instructions given to the subjects. We shall have a standardized set of instructions about the completion of the test itself. These can probably be taken directly from the test manual and will obviously be held *constant* across all subjects. The question is, how much do we tell the subjects about the aims of the experiment and about the noise itself? Here again we have to thi[illegible]out the conclusions we wish to draw. If our results are t[illegible] what happens when people perform mental tasks [illegible]tural' conditions of noise, it would be best *not* to alert [illegible]jects to the fact that we are actually studying this [illegible]em. Otherwise we may induce unnatural reactions, such as [illegible]ncreased effort to overcome the effects of noise, or even a [illegible]ightened sensitivity to noise. The best strategy is to say something general at the outset, e.g. 'We are investigating the way people solve logical reasoning problems of various kinds.' After the experiment we can, of course, reveal the true nature of the study. Indeed it is a matter of etiquette that we should do so, provided the subject is at all interested. But during the experiment itself the best policy is to keep the subject 'naive' with regard to the aims of the experiment. This means, in the present case, that the tape recorded 'noises' should appear to be perfectly natural, and not contrived for the experiment, otherwise our subjects will quickly guess what we are up to, however carefully we word the instructions.

These examples should give you a reasonable idea of the steps that must be taken to plan the *procedure* of an experiment after the basic design has been chosen. Many of the details of procedure will be settled quite arbitrarily, and will appear rather trivial. Nevertheless, it is most important that these details be permanently recorded so that other researchers can come along and check our findings, or search for an explanation as to why an apparently similar experiment has produced contradictory results.

(4) Having framed a prediction, designed an experiment, and settled the details of procedure, we are now ready to go ahead and run the experiment itself. Some hours, days or even weeks later we will have produced some figures or *data* representing the performance of each subject under the various conditions of the experiment. These are our *results*.

There are two distinct aspects to the treatment of results. First we want to display the important features of the data in a clear and precise form. This is the province of *descriptive statistics*. Secondly we want to interpret the data, i.e. use them to decide whether the experimental effect we predicted has actually occurred. This is the province of *inductive* or *inferential statistics.* In this chapter we shall focus on the description of data, but many of the concepts and tools to be developed will be important for our understanding of statistical inference, which is discussed in later sections.

Descriptive statistics, I: organizing the data

Raw data

Having completed our experiment on traffic noise we shall have two sets of figures representing the scores of experimental and control subjects on the logical reasoning test. These are the *raw* data – 'raw' because nothing has been done to extract any meaning from the numbers (see table 5).

Table 5 Hypothetical raw data for an experiment on the effects of traffic noise

Scores on logical reasoning test (maximum 20) for subjects exposed to two levels of traffic noise

Experimental group (high noise level)	*Control group (minimal noise level)*
5	15
12	11
13	12
10	13
7	10
9	14
10	12
12	13
8	9
6	11
10	13
9	14
14	12
8	12
11	10
9	11
11	13
13	9
10	12
12	14

With as many as twenty scores in each set it is very difficult to get the 'feel' of the data merely by inspecting a long column of figures. With a little effort we can discover that the lowest score in the control group is 9, and that the highest is 15. But it is difficult to see how the scores are distributed between these two numbers. Are they spread evenly between 9 and 15? Are the scores 'bunched' in the middle, around 12? Or what? Obviously we can't tell this by looking at the haphazard arrangement of scores in table 5. We need a more readily comprehensible format for the data.

Frequency distribution

Looking at the scores in more detail it can be seen that some values occur more than once. For example, in the control group four subjects achieve a score of 13; that is, the *frequency* of occurrence of the score 13 is 4. This is a clue to a more economical and meaningful way of organizing the data. We can go through the various scores in order, from lowest to highest, counting how many times each score occurs. The result is a *frequency distribution*. Table 6 shows the frequency distributions for the experimental and control data. It is useful to record

Table 6 Data of table 6 reorganized in the form of frequency distributions

Experimental group		*Control group*	
Score	*Frequency*	*Score*	*Frequency*
5	1		
6	1		
7	1	9	2
8	2	10	2
9	3	11	3
10	4	12	5
11	2	13	4
12	3	14	3
13	2	15	1
14	1		
	$N=20$		$N=20$

the total number of observations (N) at the foot of the frequency column. Of course N equals the sum of the frequencies.

Now looking at the data of table 6 we get a much clearer impression of the characteristics of each set of scores, and of the relationship between the two sets. Thus we can see that the experimental group's scores fall in the range 5–14, but tend to be bunched in the centre of this range. The control group achieves somewhat higher scores (as we predicted) in the range 9–15, and are even more closely bunched around the central values. Note that this method of presenting the data retains all the information in the original table, but in a clearer and more concise form.

What would happen however if we had 100 scores in each group, and if the range of scores was much wider – say between 1 and 50? Even after the data were organized into a frequency distribution they would still be difficult to assimilate, because there would be a large number of different scores each with a very low frequency of occurrence. In this case it is usual to reclassify the data into *groups* or *classes* (e.g. 1–5, 6–10, 11–15, etc.) and to record the frequency of scores falling within each class interval. We then obtain a *grouped frequency distribution*, as illustrated in table 7.

Table 7 Hypothetical data arranged in the form of a grouped frequency distribution

Class interval	*Midpoint*	*Frequency*
1–5	3	1
6–10	8	0
11–15	13	5
16–20	18	12
21–25	23	20
26–30	28	32
31–35	33	23
36–40	38	5
41–45	43	1
46–50	48	1
		$N = 100$

Grouping the data in this way does lose us some information, i.e. the raw data cannot be recovered exactly from the frequency table. On the other hand, we do achieve a more manageable description of the data than would have been possible otherwise. It is generally agreed that the total range of scores should be divided into something like 10–15 equal-width classes to achieve the best results; this number of classes gives a reasonably accurate representation of the original data without overtaxing our ability to comprehend their features. Obviously if the range of scores in the data is below 10 anyway (as in table 6), there is no point in grouping before we construct the frequency distribution.

In setting out a grouped frequency distribution it is conventional to indicate the *midpoint* of each class of scores. The midpoint is used to represent the numerical value of all the scores in that class, for the purposes of further analysis. This is necessary because when we are working with grouped data we do not know the individual scores within each class, only the interval in which they fall.

Histograms

We can display the data in a frequency distribution even more vividly by drawing a picture of the scores. One way of doing this is to mark off a horizontal line (or axis) in units corresponding to the scores. We then draw vertical 'boxes' above each score to represent the number of times it occurs in the data. This graphical form of the frequency distribution is known as a *histogram* or *bar chart.* Figure 2 shows the data from our noise experiment in the form of two histograms which have been constructed from the frequency distributions shown in table 6. We can now see at a glance that the control scores tend to be higher than the experimental scores (i.e. further towards the right-hand end of the axis) and more closely bunched around the centre of the range.

Grouped data can also be represented in this way, except that the horizontal axis of the histogram is marked off in class intervals instead of individual scores. You could draw out a histogram for the data in table 7 as an exercise.

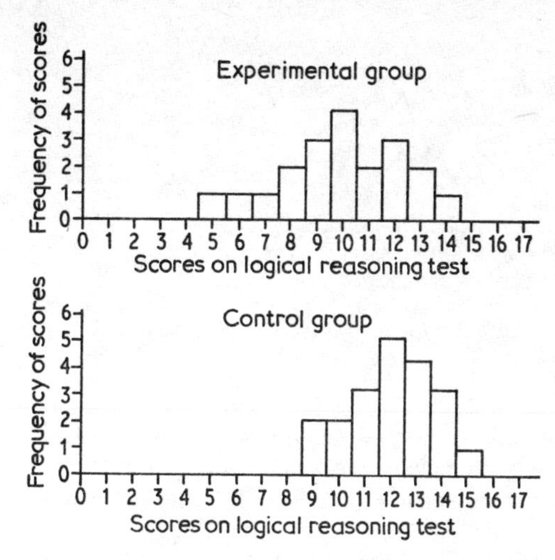

Figure 2 Histograms of the test scores of experimental and control subjects in the traffic noise experiment

Frequency polygons

If we replace the 'bars' of a histogram by dots plotted at the midpoint of the top of each bar, we have a frequency polygon. The height of the dots on the vertical axis then represents the frequency of occurrence of the scores on the horizontal axis. By joining up the dots with straight lines we obtain a very similar visual effect to that given by the histogram. There is, perhaps, a slight advantage to using frequency polygons when we want to compare two or more sets of data. This is because we can plot two frequency polygons on the same pair of axes without them interfering with each other visually. Indeed this is a very effective method of comparing two sets of data, as is shown in figure 3. Note the practice of bringing the two 'tails' of each polygon down to zero to create a neater visual effect.

Which technique should be used?

All of the above methods give a reasonably clear impression of the main features of the data, and it is largely a matter of personal preference as to which one should be used in any

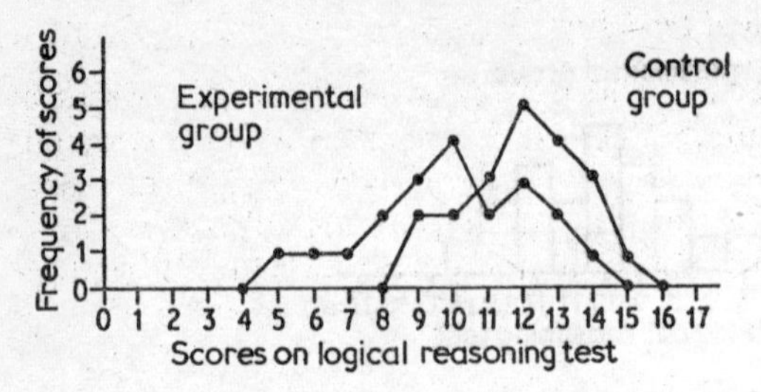

Figure 3 Frequency polygons for the test scores of experimental and control subjects in the traffic noise experiment

particular case. The only requirements are that the data should be displayed concisely, in a clearly labelled form, and in such a way that the reader can easily comprehend the pattern of results. Further details of techniques for displaying and organizing data are given in Wallis and Roberts (1963) and Blalock (1972).

Descriptive statistics, II: summarizing the data

The methods described in the previous section were simply ways of reorganizing the data with little or no loss of information. An alternative approach is to attempt to *summarize* the important features of a set of data in terms of single *measures* or *indices*. The question then is: What features of the data need to be summarized in this way? You can probably answer this question for yourself by looking back at the histograms shown in figure 2, and trying to summarize the features of each set of scores in one or two sentences. You would almost certainly want to report whereabouts on the scale from 0 to 20 most of the scores fell. This is known as the *central tendency* of the data and may be summarized by quoting a 'typical' or representative score for the whole set. A second, important feature is how widely spread the scores are on either side of the typical value; this is the *dispersion* or *variability* of the data. We may also notice other features of the distribution, such as whether its shape is symmetrical or not, but these aspects of the data are less important; for the purposes of describing our results and drawing inferences from them, we are mainly interested in central tendency and dispersion.

Measures of central tendency

How can we best characterize the typical value of a set of scores using a single figure? The answer depends to some extent on what we are going to do with the figure when we get it, and also on the *shape* of the distribution being considered. We shall now consider the three most commonly used measures of central tendency.

(1) THE MEAN

The *mean* is the technical term for what is usually called the average in everyday language. It is found by adding together every score and dividing the total by the number of scores. Thus the mean of the four scores 3, 4, 4, 6 is given by (3+4+4+6) divided by 4. This equals 17/4 or 4·25. There is really no need to say anything more about the calculation of the mean, it is so simple. However, when we come on to calculating other statistical quantities it will be extremely cumbersome to describe all the procedures in words – the operations become much too complicated for this. So we shall now introduce some statistical symbols which may appear to complicate matters at first, but which will ultimately provide you with an extremely useful shorthand for recording the steps in a piece of statistical analysis.

Returning to the definition of the mean as *the sum of all the scores divided by the number of scores*, we shall now translate this into symbols. Firstly let the symbol X stand for any score in the set; let $\bar{X}$ stand for the mean; and let N stand for the number of scores in the set. We can then rewrite our definition in the following form:

$$\bar{X} = \frac{\text{The sum of all the } X\text{s}}{N}$$

The instruction to sum all the Xs is still rather cumbersome, and we can simplify the formula even further by introducing the Greek letter sigma (Σ) to stand for the *operation* of summing a set of numbers. Hence the expression ΣX tells us to add together all the different numbers that X can stand for. Our definition of the mean then becomes:

$$\bar{X} = \frac{\Sigma X}{N}$$

As a further example, suppose our values of X are: 4, 5, 2, 4, 5. The mean of this set of scores is then given by:

$$\bar{X} = \frac{\Sigma X}{N} = \frac{4+5+2+4+5}{5} = \frac{20}{5} = 4{\cdot}0$$

(2) THE MEDIAN

The *median* is an alternative measure of the central value of a set of scores. It is defined very simply as that value which has as many scores above it as below it. Hence if our set of scores is 2, 3, 3, 5, 7, 9, 13, then 5 is the median score because it has exactly 3 scores falling above and 3 scores falling below it. If we happened to have an *even* number of scores then we define the median as the point halfway between the two middle scores. Thus the set of scores 3, 4, 5, 6, 8, 11, yields a median value of 5·5, i.e. the point halfway between 5 and 6.

It can be seen that calculating the median value of a set of scores is even simpler than finding the mean. All we have to do is to *rank* the scores in order from lowest to highest, and then read off the middle score (or the midpoint between the two middle scores if there is an even number).

(3) THE MODE

The *mode* is defined as the most frequently occurring value in a set of scores. It can be found very simply by inspection of the data. Obviously if there are only a few scores (e.g. 5, 6, 8, 3, 3) the one that occurs most frequently does not tell us very much. However, with large numbers of observations the mode becomes a somewhat more useful index of the central value of the scores.

Calculating the mean, median and mode from frequency distributions

The simple methods given above are perfectly adequate for the calculation of mean, median and mode in all circumstances. However, if you have large quantities of data, say upwards of thirty observations in each condition of an experiment, these methods become rather laborious. It is then more efficient to cast the data in the form of a frequency distribution and to calculate the measure of central tendency from this. The saving of time (and errors) is particularly marked if you are doing the calculations by hand, rather than with the aid of a calculating machine, and once the data are arranged in the form of a frequency distribution the computation of other statistics is also facilitated. The appropriate formulae and techniques are set out in detail in appendix 1 (p. 162).

Choosing between the mean, median and mode

The purpose of these measures of central tendency is to give, in a single figure, an idea of the typical value of a set of scores. (1) *When the scores are fairly symmetrically distributed about the central value* then the arithmetic average (mean), the most common score (mode), and the middle score in the sequence from low to high (median) will all have about the same value. This can be demonstrated visually using a histogram of the experimental scores from the traffic noise experiment on which the values of mean, median and mode have been superimposed (see figure 4). These values were calculated using the basic methods described above on the data of table 6. To check that you understand these methods you should calculate the three measures for yourself.

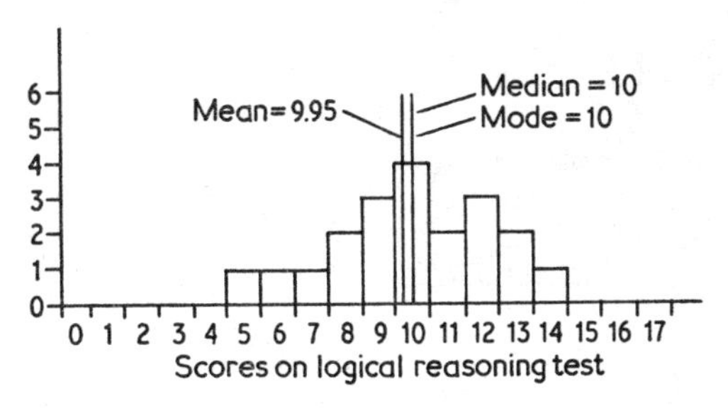

Figure 4 Histogram of the test scores of experimental subjects showing the positions of the mean, median and mode

From the point of view of *describing* the experimental results there is obviously very little to choose between the three measures of central tendency, and one would be inclined to use the one that is simplest to compute, that is, the mode. However, if we wish to undertake further analysis of these data – for example, to test the prediction that the experimental scores are significantly lower than the control scores – then the *mean* is the preferred measure of central tendency. This is because the mean summarizes *all* the data from which it is derived – a change in any one score will change the value of the mean. It is therefore a more *reliable* index of the underlying features of the data. Also the mean has certain mathematical properties which make it suitable for more advanced statistical analyses.

(2) Now let us see what happens *when the shape of the distribution of scores is markedly asymmetrical.* The technical term for this is *skewness.* A distribution may be skewed in either of two directions: *positively* skewed if the right-hand tail is extended and *negatively* skewed if the left-hand tail is extended (see figure 5).

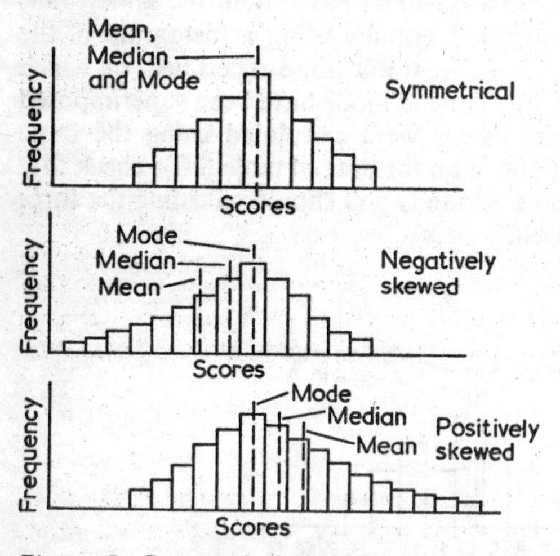

Figure 5 Symmetrical and skewed distributions and the three measures of central tendency

The effect of skewness is to separate out the three measures of central tendency. As can be seen, the mode stays at the 'peak' of the distribution irrespective of its shape. The mean moves a considerable distance outwards in the direction of the extended tail. And the median falls between the mean and the mode.

We can see why this happens by considering the following two distributions:

(*a*) 76, 77, 78, 78, 79, 80
(*b*) 1, 3, 76, 77, 78, 78, 79, 80

Distribution (*a*) is symmetrical and the mean, median and mode all have the value 78. Distribution (*b*) has been given an extended left hand tail relative to (*a*), i.e. it is negatively skewed. Now in (*b*) the mode is still 78, the most frequent score. But the mean, which is the average of all the scores, is naturally pulled down by the introduction of the two low values; it is now 59. The median is also lowered, but only to 77·5. But note that this reduction in the value of the median is not influenced by the particular values of the two low scores, only by their effect on the *position* of the middle item. In the case of a highly skewed distribution, such as (*b*), this insensitivity to extreme values is helpful; the median still retains the characteristic of being a 'typical' or central value, whereas the mean gives a misleading picture of the typical value because it is very sensitive to the value of extreme scores. Hence for highly skewed distributions the *median* is the preferred measure of central tendency.

The mode is useful whenever a quick but very approximate index of central tendency is needed. Since its value depends on just a few of the scores it cannot be regarded as a very stable measure of the features of the data; indeed, if an experiment is repeated a number of times the modal score will tend to vary much more from occasion to occasion than the mean or even the median. Hence the mode is used infrequently in psychological research.

Measures of dispersion

The second important feature of a set of scores in the extent to which they are spread out on either side of the central value. Looking back at the data from the traffic noise experiment (figure 2) we can see two different levels of dispersion; the control data are closely packed around the central values, whereas the experimental scores are more widely dispersed. This difference in dispersion is quite independent of any differences that may exist in central tendency. The control group could have had an identical *mean* score to the experimental group, but this would have no bearing on the relative *dispersion* of the two sets of scores.

Our interest in dispersion cannot be explained quite as easily as our interest in central tendency. After all, most psychological predictions relate to an expected difference between the central tendency of two groups (e.g. traffice noise produces *lower* reasoning performance than no noise), so it is obvious that we need to devise measures like the mean and median to test such hypotheses. But why do we need to describe the dispersion in a set of scores?

The answer is that we need to know the dispersion of two sets of scores in order to evaluate a predicted difference between their *means.* This will become clearer in the next chapter when we discuss inferential statistics. For the time being we can appreciate, perhaps intuitively, that if each group of scores is widely dispersed we can place little reliance on any given difference between the means; it is likely to have arisen just by chance. However, if each group of scores is fairly homogeneous, a given difference becomes that much more convincing, i.e. it is likely to be fundamental to the two conditions of the experiment rather than just a chance affair. This is why we need some way of measuring the amount of *variation* or dispersion in the data. We shall now consider the various alternatives.

THE RANGE

The most obvious index of spread is the range of values covered by the scores. Thus inspection of figure 2 tells us immediately that the range of the experimental scores is 9 points (the highest score, 14, minus the lowest score, 5). Similarly the range of the control scores is 6 (15 minus 9). This measure is very simple to derive and it can be readily understood, but there are occasions when it gives a very misleading impression of spread. Consider the following two distributions arranged in order from lowest to highest scores:

(*a*) 62, 63, 63, 64, 65, 66, 67
(*b*) 62, 64, 65, 65, 66, 67, 85

Distribution (*a*) has a range of 5 whereas distribution (*b*), because of a single unusually high score, has a range of 23 – a figure which is quite atypical of the variability in most of the data. Hence the range suffers from being sensitive *only* to the two extreme values, telling us nothing about the variability of the scores in between.

THE INTERQUARTILE RANGE

We can overcome some of the instability of the simple range by employing the interquartile range, which is effectively the range of the middle half of the scores. This is calculated by arranging the scores in order from lowest to highest and then finding the difference between the score 25 per cent of the way along the series (the first quartile) and the score 75 per cent of the way along (the third quartile). These scores are found using the same procedures as were outlined for finding the median which is, of course, the point 50 per cent of the way through the series of scores.

The difference between the first and third quartiles is a somewhat more stable measure of dispersion than the range, but it still makes use of only a small proportion of the information in the data. Furthermore, the interquartile range does not possess the mathematical properties needed for more complex statistical analysis. We shall therefore move on to more acceptable measures of dispersion.

THE MEAN DEVIATION

Suppose we want our measure of dispersion to reflect the distance of *every* observation from the mean of the scores, rather than just the distance of two arbitrarily chosen points. The simplest way to do this would be to calculate the distance between each observation and the mean, and then to find the average of all these distances. This is precisely the definition of the mean deviation. In symbols this is:

$$\text{Mean deviation} = \frac{\Sigma|X - \bar{X}|}{N}$$

where X stands for any score, $\bar{X}$ for the mean of the scores, and N for the number of scores. The symbol Σ tells us to *add* together all individual deviations between each score and the mean. The two vertical lines $|\quad|$ tell us to take the *absolute* value of the difference between each score and the mean and *not* to treat some of these differences as negative. Obviously if we did not do this then the positive deviations of all those scores above the mean would exactly cancel out with the negative deviations of all those below the mean.

We can demonstrate the calculation of this measure on the following data: 5, 7, 6, 7, 9, 8. The mean of these scores is:

$$\bar{X}=\frac{\Sigma X}{N}=\frac{42}{6}=7$$

Hence the sum of the deviations from the mean is given by:

$$\begin{aligned}\Sigma|X-\bar{X}| &= |5-7|+|7-7|+|6-7|+|7-7|+|9-7|+|8-7| \\ &= 2+0+1+0+2+1=6\end{aligned}$$

Thus, the mean deviation $=\frac{\Sigma|X-\bar{X}|}{N}=\frac{6}{6}=1$

We now have a potentially useful measure of dispersion; it takes account of all the data, it is easily calculated, and it is easy to interpret. Thus we can summarize the amount of dispersion in the above data by saying that on average the scores differ from the mean by one unit. This even 'feels' right when we look at the original set of scores. However, this is another case of a measure which lacks the mathematical properties we need for statistical inference. Returning to the earlier point that measures of dispersion are used to help us evaluate the difference between the *means* of two groups, it turns out that the mean deviation cannot be used for this purpose. In fact it is rarely used at all.

THE VARIANCE

We noted in the previous section that the quantity $(X-\bar{X})$, the difference between each score and the mean, is sometimes negative and sometimes positive, so that the deviations will tend to cancel each other out. This problem was overcome by taking only the absolute value of the deviations, and ignoring the signs. An alternative approach would be to square each deviation, thereby making the negative ones positive, and then add together the *squared* deviations. This leads to an alternative measure of dispersion known as the *variance*. The formula for the variance is:

$$\text{Variance}=\frac{\Sigma(X-\bar{X})^2}{N}$$

In words this amounts to: (1) squaring the deviations between each score and the mean, (2) adding together the squared deviations, and (3) dividing by N, the number of observations. This gives us the *mean squared deviation* rather than the more simple mean deviation which was discussed above.

Now, like the mean deviation, the variance takes account of every individual score in representing the amount of spread in the data. But, unlike the mean deviation (and the range for that matter), it has no obvious practical meaning. It is simply an abstract measure which increases as the amount of dispersion in the data increases. If all the scores were the same, the variance would be zero. And if one set of scores has a variance twice as large as a second set of scores we can say that it has twice the variability or spread. But we cannot actually attach a simple meaning to a particular variance. We cannot say that, because the variance is 3, the average deviation of a score from the mean is 3. Nor can we make any other simple statement from a knowledge of the variance. This is something that often puzzles newcomers to statistics. Since the meaning of the term is difficult to grasp intuitively you may wonder why the variance has become the most important and frequently used measure of dispersion. The answer to this question will be considered in some detail in the final section of this chapter. For the time being we shall simply note that the variance, or more correctly the *square root* of the variance, known as the *standard deviation*, can often be used to determine what proportion of a distribution of scores falls between any given pair of values. As we shall see, this facility is immensely important for testing predictions about the difference between two sets of scores. Before expanding on these ideas we shall consider the mechanics of calculating the variance and standard deviation.

Calculating the variance and standard deviation

We have defined the variance as the mean squared deviation – in symbols:

$$\frac{\Sigma(X-\bar{X})^2}{N}$$

In practice the square root of this quantity, the standard deviation, is used just as frequently as the variance to measure dispersion. Obviously it doesn't matter particularly which index is used; we can get from one to the other quite easily. But it is important that we indicate clearly in each case which one we are referring to. We shall use the symbol S^2 to denote the variance of a set of scores, and S to denote the standard deviation. Remember both of these measures will increase with the amount of spread in the data, and both will be zero when there is no spread – that is, when all the scores are the same. We have to get used to these two related measures since they are both in common use. In the same way that you might describe the size of a square either by its area, say 9 cm^2, or by the length of its side, 3 cm, so we can describe dispersion either by the variance or the standard deviation. Both measures reflect the same basic notion of dispersion.

To calculate the variance from the above formula would be a rather laborious task because it would involve subtracting the mean from every individual score X, and then squaring the results of each subtraction. Since the mean may turn out to be a number containing several decimals, this formula can lead to some complex arithmetic. Fortunately there is an alternative version of the formula which allows us to square each value of X as it is, to add the squares, and then to subtract the square of the mean just *once* at the end of the computation. This formula is:

$$\text{Variance} = S^2 = \frac{\Sigma X^2}{N} - \bar{X}^2$$

In words, this formula tells us to: (1) square each value of X, (2) add the squares together, (3) divide the sum of squares by N, the number of observations, and (4) subtract the mean squared. The use of this formula, and a convenient way of setting out the calculations, is shown in table 8 for a set of imaginary scores. Note that it is, of course, necessary to compute the mean before the variance or standard deviation can be found.

A NOTE ON THE INTERPRETATION OF ΣX^2

When we met the term ΣX in connection with the mean its interpretation was fairly obvious – add together every value of X. But the term ΣX^2 could, on the face of it, mean either of two things. It could tell us to add together every value of X and *then square* the total. Or it could tell us to square each value of X, and *then add* the squares. Some students get confused between these

Table 8 Computation of variance and standard deviation: basic method

Scores X	Scores squared X^2
12	144
14	196
16	256
14	196
13	169
15	225
18	324
$\Sigma X = 102$	$\Sigma X^2 = 1510$

Mean

$$\bar{X} = \frac{\Sigma X}{N} = \frac{102}{7} = 14{\cdot}571$$

Variance

$$S^2 = \frac{\Sigma X^2}{N} - \bar{X}^2$$

$$= \frac{1510}{7} - 14{\cdot}571^2$$

$$= 215{\cdot}714 - 212{\cdot}314$$

$$= 3{\cdot}40$$

Standard deviation (if required)

$$S = \sqrt{3{\cdot}40} = 1{\cdot}84$$

two interpretations. It is the *second* one that is correct; square each X and *then* add the squares. If we wanted to add first and then square, the appropriate expression would be $(\Sigma X)^2$.

Calculating the variance from a frequency distribution

We mentioned earlier, when discussing the mean, that large quantities of data can be processed more efficiently if the scores are set out in the form of a frequency distribution, and calculations are based on this format. The appropriate techniques for calculating the variance and standard deviation from a frequency distribution are given in appendix 2 (p. 168).

Descriptive statistics, III: the normal distribution

So far we have discussed various ways of organizing and summarizing the data obtained from a psychological experiment. We have made no assumptions about the type of distribution that could arise; instead we have focused on the simple description of whatever data happen to emerge from our study. Perhaps you are now wondering whether the shape of a distribution of scores is likely to fluctuate wildly from one experiment to another, or whether there are basic patterns that tend to recur time and again in the measurement of behaviour. Certainly the central tendency and the dispersion of the data will change from one study to another, but there is a basic *shape* which does tend to recur in the distributions of many different sorts of data. This shape is known as the *normal distribution* and is illustrated in figure 6. As you can see, it is a symmetrical distribution of scores with most values falling in the central region of the curve (i.e. near the mean) and the frequency of scores falling off fairly rapidly on either side of the central area. The general shape of the curve is sometimes described as bell-shaped, and because it is symmetrical, the mean, median and mode will all have the same value.

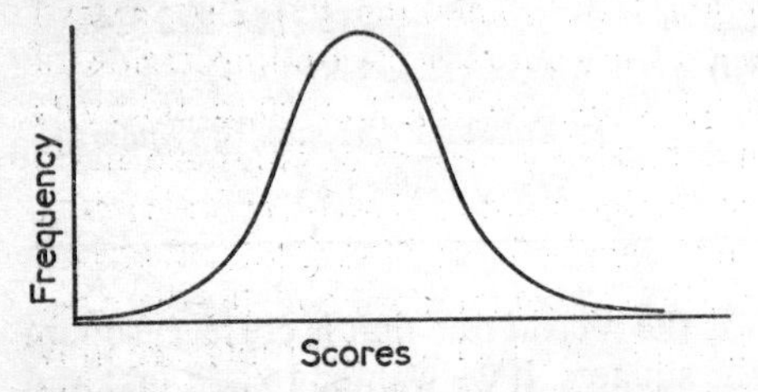

Figure 6 The normal distribution curve

The significance of the normal distribution

There are a number of reasons for paying particular attention to this type of distribution. First, the curve is interesting because so many different variables – psychological, physical and biological – have normal, or close to normal, distributions. We know, for example, that such diverse characteristics as height, intelligence, and the life of electric lamps all follow a normal curve. Secondly, the normal distribution has some very interesting and useful properties which help us in the description of data and in the interpretation of standard deviations. And thirdly, the distribution is basic to the formulation of many of the statistical tests we shall be considering in later chapters. Before expanding on the descriptive uses of this distribution we shall consider precisely what the curve represents.

The normal curve as a limiting frequency distribution

If normal distributions are so ubiquitous you may be wondering why none of the data we have discussed so far conforms to the smooth curve shown in figure 6. The reason is that we have been concerned with finite numbers of observations, whereas the normal curve represents an 'ideal' distribution which would be obtained from an indefinitely large (i.e. infinite) number of observations. It is patently obvious that we could never attain this ideal, but we can grasp the concept by imagining a histogram in which more and more observations are added to the distribution and in which the width of the class intervals is continuously reduced. Suppose, for example, we measured the heights of 100 male adults and grouped the data into a frequency distribution involving five intervals. A histogram of this distribution might look something like that shown in figure 7(a). We could gain a more accurate impression of the distribution of heights by making the class intervals narrower – which would make the measurement scale more sensitive – and by increasing the number of cases, N. This might produce the distribution shown in figure 7(b). (Note. If we had narrowed the class intervals *without* increasing N, the distribution would assume an irregular shape.) A further increase in N accompanied by a further narrowing of class intervals would produce the distribution shown in figure 7(c), and so on. It can be seen that this process leads to closer and closer approximations to the smooth curve which has been drawn through the midpoints of the top of each bar. And we can now imagine that, if we went on doing this indefinitely, we would produce the smooth curve itself, which is therefore known as the *limiting* frequency distribution. The normal curve is an example of one particular limiting frequency distribution, but, as we have said, a rather important one.

When histograms were first discussed earlier in this chapter (p. 26) we defined the *height* of each bar as being proportional to the frequency of observations within that interval. However, since the widths of the bars are all equal we can also use the *area* of each one to represent frequency. And if we regard the total area of the histogram as representing all the observations, then the area of each bar represents the *proportion* of observations falling in that particular interval. In the same way we can regard the *area* under the normal curve as representing 100 per cent of the cases in the distribution, and the area between any two vertical lines will represent the proportion of cases falling within

those limits. Hence the shaded area in figure 8 represents the proportion of adult males whose heights are within the range 70–72 inches. This interpretation of the area under a curve is used repeatedly in various aspects of statistics.

Areas under the normal curve and the standard deviation

The interesting thing about the normal curve is that there are only two things we need to know in order to draw it – its mean and its standard deviation. In other words, the equation giving the height of the curve (y) for any particular point on the horizontal axis (x) can be solved provided that we know the values of the mean and the standard deviation. The practical significance of this point is that once we know a variable is normally distributed, with a particular mean and standard deviation, we have a perfect description of the entire distribution. We can, in effect, specify precisely what proportion of the observations will fall between any two values we care to specify.

To be more specific, all normal distributions have the following property: *if we draw a vertical line a fixed number of standard deviations above the mean, we shall cut off a constant proportion of the distribution of scores.* For example, a line one standard deviation above the mean cuts off the upper 15·87 per cent of the scores; a line two standard deviations above the mean cuts off the top 2·28 per cent of the scores; a line three standard deviations above the mean cuts off 0·13 per cent, and so on. For any number (integral or otherwise) of standard deviations above the mean it is possible to specify what proportion of scores fall above this value, and what proportion fall below it (since the total area covers 100 per cent of the scores). Also, since the curve is symmetrical, a line drawn a given distance *below* the mean will cut off the same proportion of scores as one drawn that distance *above* the mean. These relationships are illustrated in figure 9. Fortunately we do not have to rely on measuring areas from a graph to determine the appropriate proportion of scores falling above any point. These figures have been worked out mathematically and are readily available in the form of a table of areas under the normal curve (see pp. 172–3).

We can now begin to appreciate the descriptive uses of the normal distribution. First, it provides a useful basis for

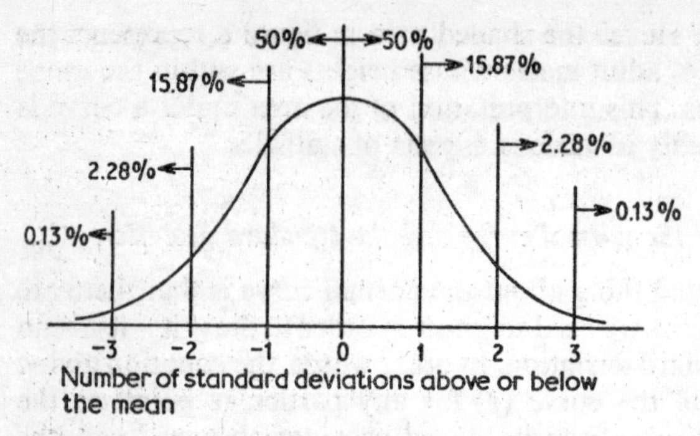

Figure 9 Proportion of scores falling above and below particular values in the normal distribution

visualizing the meaning of the standard deviation. Previously we said this measure of dispersion was entirely abstract, but this was not quite true. We now know that, provided a distribution is normal, or approximately normal, the standard deviation tells us what proportion of scores fall within any particular limits we are interested in. Using figure 9 we can see that approximately two-thirds of the scores will fall within one standard deviation on each side of the mean. So we now have a more concrete way of thinking about the standard deviation of a set of scores.

Secondly, the properties we have just outlined enable us to answer practical questions about a set of scores with great ease. Suppose we know that the heights of adult males are normally distributed with a mean of 68 inches and a standard deviation of 2·5 inches; we can now discover exactly what proportion of people will be, say, 70 inches or taller. We proceed as follows: (1) 70 inches is 2 inches above the mean of 68 inches; (2) 2 inches is 0·8 of a standard deviation (since $S = 2{\cdot}5$ inches); (3) so our question becomes: What proportion of a normal distribution falls beyond 0·8 standard deviations from the mean? Our table of areas under the normal curve tells us that this proportion is 21·19 per cent. Note that all we had to do to solve this problem was to *transform* the score we were interested in to a distance from the mean measured in units of standard deviation. This distance is known as a Z score and may be expressed algebraically as:

$$Z = \frac{X - \bar{X}}{S}$$

where X is the score, $\bar{X}$ the mean, and S the standard deviation.

Now suppose we are interested in the proportion of people who will have heights between, say, 63 and 66 inches. We can answer this question by finding the proportion of scores below 63 inches, the proportion below 66 inches, and subtracting the first proportion from the second. Thus 63 inches is two standard deviations below the mean ($Z = (63-68)/2{\cdot}5$). From the tables we discover that 2·28 per cent of cases fall below this value of Z. The height of 66 inches is 0·8 standard deviations below the mean ($Z = (66-68)/2{\cdot}5$). We already know that 21·19 per cent of cases fall below this value of Z. So the proportion of people with heights between 63 and 66 inches will be (21·19 − 2.28 per cent) which is 18·91 per cent (see figure 10).

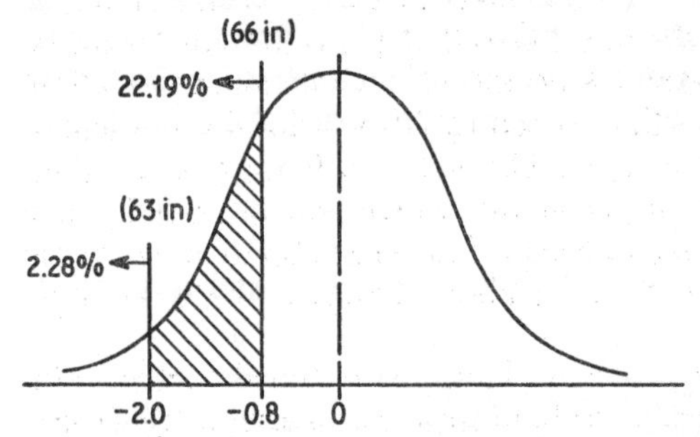

Figure 10 Proportion of cases falling between two values in a normal distribution of heights

As a final example, suppose we wish to know which height is so extreme that only 10 per cent of people will fall beyond this value. To solve this problem we have to work backwards from the general properties of normal distributions to specific features of our height distribution. Firstly we use the normal tables to find out how many standard deviations above the mean we have to go to cut off the upper 10 per cent of cases. The appropriate Z value is 1·28. Since the standard deviation of height is 2·5 inches, the tallest 10 per cent of people will have heights at least $1{\cdot}28 \times 2{\cdot}5$ ($=3{\cdot}2$) inches above the mean. Hence the height we require is 71·2 inches. (Note: This result could have been obtained by substituting $Z=1{\cdot}28$, $S=2{\cdot}5$ and $\bar{X}=68$ in the above formula and solving for X.)

Another way of expressing the result we have just obtained is to say that there is a 10 per cent chance, or a probability of 0·1, that a person picked at random from the population of adult males will be 71·2 inches or more in height. This shift from proportions to probabilities is important when we come to use the normal distribution to evaluate the significance of the difference between two means. Then we shall be asking such questions as: What is the probability that two means would differ by such an amount just by chance? The normal distribution can help us to answer such questions in certain circumstances. But this will be discussed more fully in chapter 4. In this section our purpose was simply to establish the properties of the normal distribution and to show how it can be used to provide very precise descriptive information about data which is known to approximate to the normal distribution.

Chapter summary

1 There are four major steps in the design and analysis of experiments:

   1 Stating the prediction to be tested.
   2 Selecting an appropriate experimental design.
   3 Operationalizing the experiment.
   4 Analysing the results.

2 The analysis of results may be subdivided into *descriptive statistics* (displaying the important features of the data) and *inferential statistics* (deciding whether the results confirm the predicted effects of the independent variable).
3 Descriptive statistics involves the *organization* of data in a readily comprehensible form. This may be achieved by retabulating the raw data in a systematic form such as a *frequency distribution*, or using graphical methods such as the *histogram* and *frequency polygon.*
4 A second function of descriptive statistics is to *summarize* important features of the data using numerical *indices*. The

most important features of a set of scores are the *central tendency* (the 'typical' or central value) and the *dispersion* (the amount of spread or variability).

5 The three most commonly used measures of central tendency are the *mean* (arithmetical average), the *mode* (most common score), and the *median* (middle score in the sequence from low to high). When the distribution of scores is fairly symmetrical these three measures have approximately equal values. In this case the mean is the most useful and reliable index of central tendency. However, if the distribution of scores is markedly asymmetrical (i.e. *skewed*), the median gives a more reasonable indication of the typical value.

6 The dispersion in a set of scores may be measured by the *range* (difference between the lowest and highest scores), the *interquartile range* (range of the middle half of the scores), the *mean deviation* (the average deviation between each score and the mean), and the *variance* (the average of the squared deviations between each score and the mean). The variance, and its square root, the *standard deviation*, are the most useful indices of dispersion because of their relationship to the normal distribution.

7 The *normal curve* is a symmetrical, bell-shaped frequency distribution which is found to fit fairly closely many real distributions of psychological and other variables. The curve is completely defined by its mean and standard deviation, and the standard deviation has a special relationship to the area under the curve; a fixed proportion of the curve falls beyond any value which is expressed in terms of its deviation from mean, measured in units of standard deviation.

8 This property is useful both in the analysis and description of real distributions of data, and in the formulation of many of the statistical tests to be considered in later chapters.

3

Basic concepts of statistical testing

Statistical inference

In the mind of the layman the field of statistics is normally associated with the collection of great volumes of numerical information which is subsequently tabulated, charted and summarized in various ways. Hence we learn of the 'average number of children in a British family', or the 'median wage of industrial workers in south-east England'. To be sure, the use of statistics to *describe* large collections of numerical information is perfectly legitimate. Indeed the psychologist takes over these methods of description when presenting the results of his experiments, as we saw in the last chapter. But we also use statistics in a much more fundamental way to draw *inferences* from the results of an experiment. We don't simply want to report the scores of our two groups of subjects, or to give the mean and standard deviation and leave it at that. We want to use the data to *test* our original prediction – to decide whether the independent variable is having the effect we supposed, or whether, perhaps, there is no real difference between the performance of the two groups. This is the function of *inferential statistics*.

To see more precisely what we mean by this term let us return to our imaginary experiment on the effects of noise on mental performance. Our prediction was that subjects exposed to traffic noise (the experimental group) would produce lower scores on a logical reasoning test than those who worked in quieter surroundings (the control group). To test this prediction or *experimental hypothesis* we obtained the scores of the two groups, which were presented in table 6 (p. 23). The scores of the control subjects do indeed seem to be higher on *average*, but we can see from the frequency polygons of figure 3 (p. 28) that there is considerable *overlap* between the two sets of scores. This leaves us in a quandary; if the experimental subjects had all scored around 5 on the reasoning test, and the control subjects had all produced scores of 15 or 16, we would almost certainly decide that our prediction was correct – that noise really does impair mental performance in this particular task. But the results are not that clear cut. We can't say, just by looking at the data, that there is obviously a difference between the groups *due to the independent variable.*

Why can't we say this? After all, there is *some* difference between the two sets of scores. What else could have caused this, other than the independent variable? To answer these questions let us look at the variation *within* each set of scores. This variation cannot be due to the independent variable, because, within a group, the independent variable is constant. We know from chapter 1 that the random variation within a set of scores is caused by *irrelevant variables* that have not been held constant, for example, differences between subjects or between testing conditions. Now if the subjects in the control group differ among themselves, and the subjects in the experimental group differ among themselves, then it is possible that the *average* characteristics of the two groups will also differ from *each other*. For example, perhaps the control group happens to contain some slightly more intelligent subjects, or maybe the cubicles used to test the control subjects were, on average, a bit cooler than those used by the experimental group. Remember that even if we randomize the effects of irrelevant variables, we cannot guarantee that these effects will balance out perfectly between the two groups (see p. 14). So the problem before us is to decide (1) whether the superior performance of the control group was caused simply by irrelevant variables that did not quite balance out in the randomization process, or (2) whether the difference between the groups is so large that it must have been caused by the difference in noise levels, i.e. the independent variable.

This is the fundamental issue in statistical inference, and it is important that you understand it fully before proceeding to the mechanics of statistical testing. We shall therefore repeat the above argument in a slightly different, but logically equivalent, form. When comparing the scores of two groups of subjects we wish to know whether the differences have been caused by the independent variable. We would not expect the two sets of scores to be absolutely identical – there are bound to be some differences *just by chance*. The problem for statistical inference is to decide whether the *actual* differences are caused by chance, or whether these differences are so large that we can ascribe them, at least in part, to the effects of the independent variable. In this description of statistical inference we are using the word 'chance' as a shorthand for 'the effects of irrelevant variables that are not perfectly matched across the two groups'. We shall continue to use the term in this sense.

To sum up, then, we shall be using statistical inference to infer from the data whether the predicted effect of the independent variable actually occurred in the experiment. We are making inferences from observable data to causal relationships between variables.

Significance level

Let us immediately qualify the impression you may have gained that we can actually decide whether the difference between our two sets of scores was caused by the independent variable or by chance factors. We would like to make a categorical decision of this kind, but the logic of scientific method does not allow us to do so. We can never prove *beyond any doubt* that chance was *not* responsible for the superior performance of the control group. Even if every control subject far surpassed the performance of every experimental subject, the sceptic could still justifiably claim that we happened – just by chance – to allocate the most intelligent twenty subjects to the control group. We would then claim that the allocation was made completely at random, but he could again reply that using a random procedure the most intelligent subjects *would* end up in the control group once in 780 times, just by chance (this probability may be found using elementary probability theory; see Kolstoe, 1973). Maybe our experiment happens to be that one time in 780. At this point we should have to admit defeat. It is, indeed, just possible that even a very marked difference between the two sets of scores could happen by chance.

Accepting, then, that we cannot prove beyond *any* doubt that the independent variable was responsible for the differences between our two groups, can we prove beyond *reasonable* doubt that this was the case? This is precisely what statistical testing tells us. By conducting a statistical test on the data of an experiment we shall be able to say *how likely it is that any given difference is due to chance.* If it is very *unlikely* that the difference could be caused by chance – say the *probability* is one in 780 – then we would conclude that the independent variable is responsible for the difference. The difference is then said to be *significant.* If, on the other hand, the difference between the two groups could easily have arisen by chance, then there is no reason to ascribe it to the effect of the independent variable. The findings are *non-significant.* Naturally we usually hope for significance, since this implies that our prediction is correct.

Now, you may ask, how unlikely must the chance explanation be before we reject it, and regard the results as significant? This is essentially an arbitrary matter – a matter of convention rather than basic principle. Most experimental psychologists choose a *significance level* of 0·05 or 1/20. This means that a difference between two groups will be assumed to reflect chance factors *unless* the results could only arise by chance one time in twenty, or less. However, in certain circumstances – for example, when our prediction contradicts an established theory – we may set outselves more demanding levels of significance, say 0·01 or even 0·001, so as to be that much more confident in any findings that reach our chosen level of significance.

Statistical tests

If you have properly understood the concepts presented in the previous section you should be in a good position to master the practical aspects of statistical testing that are to follow. A statistical test is simply a device for calculating the likelihood that our results are due to chance fluctuations between the groups. Different tests calculate this likelihood in different ways, depending on the design of the experiment and the nature of the dependent variable. But these are technical – almost trivial – matters. You need to master them in the same way that you need to select and use the right tools to repair a car. But the basic principle of statistical testing – analogous to knowing how a car works – has already been covered. In the sections that follow we shall try to maintain this distinction between the principle of assessing the probability that chance factors can explain the results, and the mechanics of actually measuring this probability.

The terminology of statistical testing

Probability

What do we mean when we say that the probability (p) of getting our results by chance is, for example, 0·25? Well, the probability of an event is the likelihood that it will occur, expressed on a scale ranging from 0 to 1; 0 represents no chance of it occurring and 1 means that it is certain to occur. The above statement would then imply that if chance alone were operating our results would occur one in four times over a very large number of replications of the experiment. This is all that statistical testing can tell us. We then have to decide whether a p value of 0·25 is *low* enough for us to conclude that chance factors did *not* produce the results obtained in our experiment. As we saw in the last section, this p value is not low enough. We only reject the chance explanation when it is extremely improbable, i.e. when p is less than or equal to 0·05. (Note: we can express this as $p \leqslant 0{\cdot}05$; similarly, p greater than or equal to 0·05 is written $p \geqslant 0{\cdot}05$.)

Null and alternate hypothesis

We have represented the process of statistical inference as deciding between two competing explanations of the difference between our two sets of scores:

1 The differences arise because of purely chance fluctuations in the two groups of scores.

2 The differences are caused, at least in part, by the independent variable.

It is rather cumbersome to spell out these explanations in detail every time we wish to refer to them. Instead we shall use the conventional terms *null hypothesis* and *alternate hypothesis* to refer to the first and second explanations respectively. Thus in the experiment on noise, our null hypothesis would be that there is no fundamental difference between performance under experimental and control conditions; any differences that do arise are due to chance. The alternate hypothesis is that traffic noise does cause an impairment in performance relative to the quieter, control conditions. The alternate hypothesis, therefore, corresponds to the experimenter's prediction and is sometimes called the *experimental hypothesis.*

Using this terminology, we can now say that a statistical test tells us the probability that the results could have occurred under the null hypothesis, i.e. purely by chance. The whole process of statistical inference may then be summarized as follows:

1 State the null and alternate hypotheses.
2 Calculate the probability, p, that our results could have been obtained under the null hypothesis. This involves:
   (a) Selecting the right statistical test.
   (b) Executing the test.
3 Reject null hypothesis if $p \leqslant 0{\cdot}05$ (i.e. accept the alternate hypothesis that the difference between the groups is caused by the independent variable). Do not reject null hypothesis if $p > 0{\cdot}05$.

Type I and type II errors

As we said earlier, we can never be absolutely certain about a statistical decision. Suppose we reject the null hypothesis whenever its probability of accounting for the results falls below 0·05. Most of the time we shall be making the correct decision. But occasionally we shall reject the null hypothesis when it is, in fact, correct. This is known as a *type I error.* The probability of committing such an error is actually equivalent to the significance level we select. If we reject the null hypothesis whenever the chance of it being true is less than 0·05, then obviously we shall be wrong 5 per cent of the time.

The most obvious defence against the type I error is to choose a more stringent significance level, say 0·01 or 0·001. The problem with this is that we then increase the risk of another type of error – the failure to detect significance when it is present. This is known as the *type II error*. Obviously we don't want to set the probability required for significance (usually called α) at such a low level that we rarely get the chance to reject the null hypothesis and accept a result as significant. The α value of 0·05 is normally considered to give about the right balance between the risks of these two errors.

Samples and populations

So far we have said nothing about the way in which we set about the calculation of p, the probability that our results could have been obtained purely by chance. This will be discussed fully in the next chapter, but we should introduce here some basic concepts which underlie virtually all the statistical tests you will be meeting. In particular you need to be familiar with the notions of *sample* and *population* as they are used in statistical testing.

The term population is used in statistics to refer to all possible objects of a particular type. For example, we might talk of the population of people in Great Britain, or the population of people in a particular town. But the objects in a population needn't be people, they could be measurements. Thus we might refer to the population of intelligence quotients of students in a particular university or college. It is not even necessary for the number of objects in a population to be finite, or for the objects to actually exist. Thus we have a population of all the possible outcomes to the traffice noise experiment, which is a conceptual population of scores, infinite in number.

Even if a population is of finite size, it is rarely possible to study every object within it. Imagine the time and expense involved in testing the IQs of all 10,000 students within a particular university. Instead sociologists, statisticians, market researchers and other observers of large groups take *samples* of observations from the populations of interest, from which they seek to make inferences about the populations themselves. Suppose, for example, we wished to know the average IQ of the 10,000 students mentioned above. We might select a *random* sample, i.e. one in which every student had an equal chance of being selected from the population. If the mean of the sample was 123·6 we could suppose that the mean of the population would also be around this figure. In formal terms we would be using the value of a *sample statistic* to estimate the value of a *population parameter*. Provided the sample was selected randomly this estimate would be a fair or *unbiased* one – that is, just as likely to over-estimate as underestimate the true value. But naturally the accuracy of the estimate would depend on the size of the sample; the larger the sample, the more accurate the estimate of the population mean.

Now let us consider how the notions of sample and population are used in statistical testing. When we conduct an experiment, such as the one relating noise to mental performance, we are not, in any obvious sense, collecting a random sample of scores from a real population. Nevertheless, we can make use of the properties of samples and populations in the following way.

First, it is possible to regard each set of scores as a randomly selected sample from an *imaginary* population of scores. For example, the experimental scores may be thought of as a sample from the population of scores that would be obtained if an infinite number of subjects – identical in characteristics to the forty subjects used in our experiment – were to have performed the logical reasoning test under noisy conditions. A similar, imaginary population of scores exists for the subjects tested under the quieter (control) condition. Now the means of these two populations represent the *true* levels of performance under the two conditions of the experiment; they are true measures because they summarize the performance of all the people typified by our subjects. The standard deviations of the populations represent the variability in performance caused by uncontrolled subject characteristics and situational variables.

Secondly, suppose for a moment that the null hypothesis is correct – that the difference between the two samples *is* due to chance. Another way of saying this is that the two populations defined above are, in fact, identical. The underlying distribution of scores is the same for experimental and control conditions. We can then explain the observed *difference* between the means of the two samples in terms of *sampling variability*; the fact that whenever we draw two random samples from the same population, the means of those samples are bound to vary slightly just by chance.

We have now translated our original problem – finding the probability that our two groups of scores differ by chance – into a slightly different form: namely, finding the probability that the two samples come from the same underlying population. In other words, we are now asking whether the difference between the two samples is small enough to arise from sampling variability in a single population (the null hypothesis), or whether the observed difference is so large that we must assume an underlying difference in the means of the populations from which the samples have been figuratively drawn (the alternate hypothesis). These alternatives are represented diagrammatically in figure 11.

We have already said that we make the choice between null and alternate hypotheses on the basis of the probability that our results could be obtained under the null hypothesis alone. Using the notions of sample and population, we can say that each statistical test is a means of computing the probability that two samples, which differ as much as the observed samples, could have been randomly selected from the same population of scores. The exact way in which we calculate this probability depends on the assumptions which are made about the underlying populations. We shall deal with this in the context of each statistical test.

Selecting the appropriate statistical test

There are two major factors that determine the correct test for any particular set of experimental results: (1) the research design and (2) the nature of the dependent variable, that is, the actual data. We shall now consider each of these factors in turn. The major statistical tests are classified according to these two factors in table 9.

Choosing a test to fit your design

Do not be alarmed into thinking that there is a separate test for every different method of controlling irrelevant variables: there isn't. But there are different tests for the six basic research

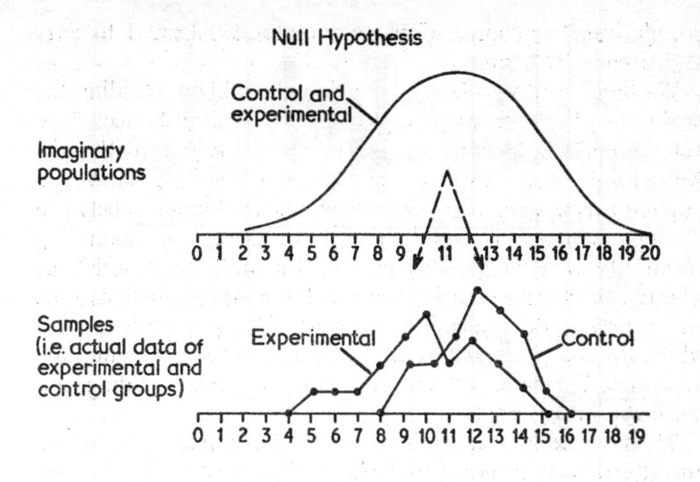

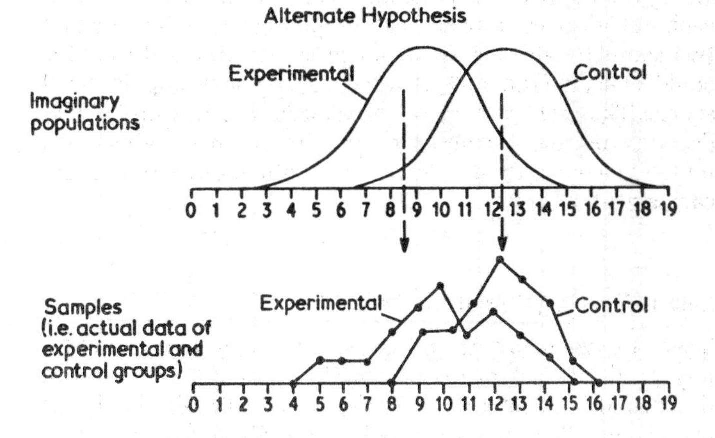

Figure 11 The relationship between samples and populations under the null and alternate hypotheses (data from the traffice noise experiment)

designs shown at the head of table 9. We give here a brief definition of each type of design, but further details are given in the appropriate chapters.

Table 9 Classification of the statistical techniques used in simple research designs

TYPE OF DATA ↕ / TYPE OF RESEARCH DESIGN ↔	*One-sample*	*Two-sample*		*k sample*		*Correlation*
		Related	*Independent*	*Related*	*Independent*	
Parametric tests	One-sample Z One-sample t	Related t	Independent Z Independent t Variance ratio (F)-test			Product–moment correlation coefficient Linear regression
Non-parametric tests	One-sample proportions test	Wilcoxon test Sign test	Mann-Whitney test χ^2 test (2×2)	Page's L trend test	Jonckheere trend test	Spearman's rank correlation coefficient

ONE-SAMPLE DESIGN

This approach is not commonly encountered in experimental research because the results may be difficult to interpret. Essentially a single sample of data is collected and this is compared with a level of performance established in previous research (or predicted by a specified theory). For example, a new method of teaching children to read may produce 60 per cent success within one year in a sample of 100 children. We can assess the effectiveness of the new method by comparing this level of performance with the previously established success rate using the old method. Thus only *one* experimental condition is needed since reading norms under the old method will have been clearly established before the study. Statistical tests for this type of design are described in chapter 6.

TWO-SAMPLE DESIGNS

This is the main focus of our attention since it is the simplest form that a true experiment can take. In a two-sample design we compare the performance of subjects under two levels of the independent variable (e.g. noise–no noise) in order to see whether the IV is affecting the subjects' behaviour. Two-sample designs are sub-divided into *related* and *independent* sample designs.

A *related samples* design is one in which some effort has been made to equate the subject characteristics influencing each set of scores. This may have been done *either* by matching pairs of subjects on appropriate variable(s) and assigning one member of each pair to each condition (the matched subjects design) *or* by using each subject twice, once in each condition, having counterbalanced the order of performance of the two conditions (the repeated measures design). The details of these procedures are described in chapter 1 (pp. 10–12). Our only concern here is to note that whenever the same set of subjects, or matched pairs, are used under the two conditions of an experiment we use the tests appropriate to related samples. These tests are also occasionally described as tests for *correlated samples* or groups.

A design is said to involve *independent samples* or independent groups when two entirely separate groups of individuals are assigned to the two conditions. In this design, subject variables are controlled by *random* allocation of subjects to the two conditions (see chapter 1, pp. 13–15). It is not even necessary for the same number of subjects to be allocated to each group, although this is usually done. Here again there is a specific set of tests appropriate to independent samples.

Tests for independent samples are described in chapters 4 (means and medians) and 7 (variances). Tests for related samples are given in chapter 5.

k SAMPLE DESIGNS

Many experiments involve comparisons between more than two conditions or levels of the independent variable. Such experiments are called *k* sample designs, where *k* can stand for any number of conditions from three upward. As with the two-sample design we may have *either* independent groups of subjects tested under each condition *or* related groups (i.e. matched sets of *k* individuals or, more likely, repeated measures on the same subjects). Different tests apply to these two cases. We have not attempted to cover the entire range of *k* sample tests, but two specific examples are described in chapter 7.

CORRELATION

A correlation is not really an experiment at all – at least not in its usual form. In a correlation the investigator *measures* the independent variable rather than manipulating it, and looks for a relationship between these measurements and the values of the dependent variable. For example, we may be interested in whether intelligence is related to how quickly people speak. We could measure both variables in a set of volunteer subjects and try to plot the relationship between these two aspects of behaviour. This situation differs from the previous examples in two respects: (1) the investigator cannot manipulate intelligence as he would in a true experiment; (2) the number of levels of the IV is completely outside our control and will depend on the particular levels of intelligence that happen to occur in our sample.

Techniques for analysing these kinds of relationships are described in chapters 8 and 9.

Choosing a test to fit the characteristics of the data

PARAMETRIC TESTS

There are basically two types of statistical test – parametric and non-parametric. *Parametric tests* are based on highly restrictive assumptions about the type of data which are obtained in the experiment: (1) it is assumed that each sample of scores has been drawn from a *normal* population; that is, if a very large number of observations was obtained under each condition of the experiment, then the resulting distributions would follow a normal curve; (2) these populations are assumed to have the same variance; (3) the variable is assumed to have been measured on an *interval* scale. We shall consider the meaning of each of these requirements in turn.

Normality How do we know, on the basis of perhaps a few observations, that our data may be regarded as a sample from a normal population? Unless the features of the data are well known from previous research (e.g. it is known that intelligence is approximately normal in distribution), there is no way we can be certain that this requirement is met. It is possible to sketch out a histogram of the data to see whether they 'look' very markedly skewed or non-normal, and we can also do a statistical test (not covered in this book) to assess whether the sample distribution is significantly different from what would have been expected using a normal population. But we cannot actually prove that a particular sample is drawn from a normal population.

Equal variances Here again it is impossible to prove that two samples come from populations with equal variances, but we can detect obvious violations of the rule. This can be done by inspection of the spread in the two sets of data, or better still, by a test designed to assess the probability that the two samples come from populations with equal variance (see the *F*-test, pp. 128–30).

Interval measurement In order to discuss this requirement for parametric tests we shall have to introduce a new concept – the idea of *levels of measurement*. Consider, for a moment, some of the different types of measure that may be used in a psychological experiment: reaction time, the number of items remembered correctly, whether a subject does one thing or another (e.g. looks directly at an interviewer or away from him), the subject's judgement of an object's size, the rating of a subject on a scale of talkativeness, or authoritarianism, and so on. The scales on which these variables are measured have different properties: that is, the numbers used to represent some variables will have more meaning than those used to represent other variables.

The *weakest* level of measurement is known as the *nominal scale*. Here we use numbers merely to classify behaviour into different classes but without implying that one class is numerically related to any other. For example, we might represent direction of gaze by the numerals 0, 1, 2, where 0 represents looking downwards, 1 represents looking upwards, and 2 represents looking directly at an interviewer. These three numbers are then being used simply to classify the responses of the subjects; it would be meaningless to say that 2 represented 'more' of something than 1 or 0, or that 1 represents the average performance of two subjects rated 0 and 2 respectively. Nominal scaling is a method of identifying *qualitatively* different responses and obviously cannot be given any quantitative meaning.

Consider now the *ranking* of a group of ten foods in order of 'tastiness' by a particular subject. We could assign the rank of 1 to the least tasty and the rank of 10 to the most tasty. Now here the numbers do have some quantitative meaning; we can say that there is more tastiness in the food ranked in position 8 than that ranked 7, and so on. But we cannot say anything about the relative differences between pairs of rankings; it would be meaningless to say that the difference in tastiness between the foods ranked 2 and 3 was equivalent to the difference in tastiness of items ranked 7 and 8. The scale simply doesn't contain such detailed information – items ranked 1 and 2 could be much closer in terms of tastiness than items ranked 7 and 8, but the measurements would not reflect this. They simply indicate the *order* of items on a particular attribute, but not their separations on the scale. Hence this level of measurement is known as *ordinal scaling*.

The highest level of measurement usually attained in psychology is known as *interval scaling*. Here we not only represent the *ordering* of items on the characteristic being measured, but also the relative *separation* of items in the scale. To take a non-psychological example, temperature as measured on the centigrade scale represents interval scaling. The three temperatures 10°C, 20°C and 30°C represent increasing levels of heat that is, they possess ordinality. But also we can say that the difference between 10° and 20° is the *same* as the difference between 20° and 30°. Hence this scale achieves an interval level of measurement. It now makes sense to use arithmetic operations on the intervals, such as addition and division. Hence we say that the average of 10° and 20° is 15° without violating the properties of the attribute being measured. In order to do this, it is clear that the measurements must be based on some agreed units such as degrees, feet, seconds, and so forth. It is the *unit* that enables us to equate intervals between points on the scale. Now it is evident that psychological variables such as intelligence, prestige or neuroticism cannot be measured in terms of established, standard units analogous to degrees or seconds. Nevertheless, under certain circumstances it is possible to make a case for a particular measurement procedure satisfying the requirements of interval scaling; such claims have been made for measures of intelligence, attitudes and other variables (see, for example, Stone and James, 1965).

In the case of variables such as reaction time, number of errors, magnitude of response, there is no question but that interval measurement has been achieved. Quite obviously we can regard the difference between $\frac{1}{2}$ second and $\frac{3}{4}$ second as equivalent to the difference between $\frac{3}{4}$ second and 1 second. Indeed such measures are said to have the characteristics of a *ratio scale*, by which we mean that one can meaningfully talk of the ratio of two measures as well as the interval between them. Thus a reaction time of 2 seconds is, in a real sense, twice as long as a reaction time of 1 second. A pressure on the response key of 3 lb is three times as great as a pressure of 1 lb, and so on. In order to make such statements it is necessary for the scale to have an absolute zero point corresponding to no time, no pressure, or whatever.

Having defined the various levels of measurement, we can now return to the measurement requirements for parametric tests. As stated above, all parametric tests assume that the data has at least interval scaling. The reason for this is that parametric tests involve the calculation of means and standard deviations – statistics that involve the addition and division of sets of numbers. As we have seen above, these operations only make sense when the numbers represent units of constant size; it does *not* make sense to add together rankings obtained from the ordering of items on a scale.

To summarize, parametric tests assume that the two samples of data are drawn from populations that have normal distributions and equal variances (sometimes called *homogeneity of variance*). It is also assumed that the dependent variable has been measured on an interval scale or a ratio scale.

NON-PARAMETRIC TESTS

In contrast, *non-parametric tests* make very few assumptions about the nature of experimental data. Most tests assume only an *ordinal level* of measurement. Suppose, for example, we wished to compare the aggressiveness ratings of two groups of subjects. Our scale of aggression might be based on the judgements of trained observers using a scale from 1 (low aggression) to 7 (high aggression). It would seem unlikely that the points on this scale are separated by equal increments in aggressiveness (interval scaling). All we are prepared to say is that the *ordering* of aggressiveness is reflected by the ratings; 7 represents more aggressiveness than 6, and so on. In this case we have an ordinal level of measurement, allowing us to use non-parametric tests, but not parametric tests. As we shall see later, some non-parametric tests even permit the testing of hypotheses about nominal data.

As far as population distributions are concerned, non-parametric tests make *no* assumptions about the shape of these distributions, nor do they assume that the two populations have equal amounts of spread. Hence these tests are sometimes referred to as *distribution-free* tests of significance. A very useful bibliography of the many non-parametric tests developed in recent years is provided by Singer (1979).

Choosing between parametric and non-parametric tests

If non-parametric tests are so generally applicable, and make relatively weak assumptions about the data, why do we not simplify matters by making exclusive use of these techniques, and ignore the parametric tests? The answer is that parametric tests are generally more *powerful* than the corresponding non-parametric tests. Loosely speaking, the power of a test is its ability to detect a significant difference between two sets of scores. The greater power of parametric tests should not be too surprising; these tests make use of *all* the information in the data, whereas the equivalent non-parametric tests simply take account of the *rank order* of the scores.

As experimenters we shall naturally wish to maximize our chances of demonstrating the effects of the independent variable. This means we shall always use a parametric test when the properties of the data allow us to do so. But what happens if one or more of the requirements of these tests is violated? Strictly speaking we should settle for the somewhat less powerful non-parametric tests. However, statisticians have recently examined what happens to the accuracy of certain parametric tests (i.e. the *t*-tests) when the basic assumptions of normality and homogeneity of variance are systematically violated. Happily these studies show that the results of the *t*-test are not seriously distorted even when quite marked departures from the basic assumptions are introduced. In this respect the *t*-test is said to be highly *robust*, and may be used generally without much attention to anything other than the most glaring departures from normality and homogeneity of variance. (There is one exception to this rule, demonstrated by Boneau (1960), who showed that very misleading results can occur when marked differences in variance occur together with unequal sample sizes. Thus, if the sample sizes are different, it is useful to check that the variances are *not* significantly different using an *F*-test (see pp. 128–30). If the difference does approach significance, it is then safer to use a non-parametric test.)

An overview

Table 9 gives a summary of the various tests to be covered in this book. Your choice is determined by the design of the experiment and the nature of the data (suitable for parametric or non-parametric tests). The way in which these classifications are made has been discussed above. However, you will see that for some conditions there are two tests listed in the table. The reasons for having two alternative tests in these cases will be given when the particular tests are discussed.

The principles underlying the selection of tests are difficult to assimilate on first presentation. We shall therefore reconsider the question of choice as we come to discuss each test in the following chapters.

Chapter summary

1 *Statistical inference* seeks to go beyond the mere description of experimental data, and to establish the *cause* of the difference between the results of the experimental and control groups.
2 There are two possible explanations for the difference between the mean performance of the two groups: (1) that the difference arises from chance factors, such as the slightly different composition of the two groups of subjects (null hypothesis); (2) that the difference is caused by the independent variable (alternate hypothesis).
3 A *statistical test* is used to determine the probability that the observed results could have occurred under the null hypothesis. If this probability is less than, or equal to, 0·05 the null hypothesis is rejected in favour of the alternate hypothesis, and the results are said to be *significant.*
4 There are two types of error that may arise in the process of statistical inference. We may decide to reject the null hypothesis when it is, in fact, correct – a type I error. Alternatively, we may decide not to reject the null hypothesis when it is false – a type II error. If we seek to reduce the risk of a type I error (by lowering the probability required for significance) we automatically increase the risk of a type II error.
5 A *population* is defined as a collection of all the possible objects, people or scores of a particular type. Statisticians use the characteristics of randomly selected *samples* to *estimate* the characteristics of the populations from which the samples have been drawn. The characteristics of a sample are known as *sample statistics.* The characteristics of a population are known as *population parameters.*
6 In *statistical testing* the two groups of data may be regarded as randomly selected samples from imaginary populations of scores. Under the null hypothesis these two populations should be identical, and the difference between the two samples is explained by *sampling variability* – the fact that any two random samples from a single population will differ

slightly just by chance. Hence a statistical test may be regarded as a means of computing the probability that the two samples have been drawn from a single population.

7 The selection of an appropriate statistical test for a two-sample experiment depends on (1) whether the samples are *related* (matched subjects and repeated measures designs) or *independent* and (2) whether the data are suitable for *parametric* or *non-parametric* tests.

8 Ideally a parametric test demands that the underlying populations of scores should be normally distributed and with equal variances. It is also assumed that the scores have been obtained from at least an *interval scale* of measurement – that is, a scale in which the distance between any two numbers is made up of units of known size.

9 A non-parametric test makes no assumptions about the shape or variability of the population distributions. The *level of measurement* required is usually *ordinal* – that is, the numbers need only represent the rank order of objects on a scale from high to low.

10 Parametric tests are to be preferred to non-parametric tests because of their greater *power* to detect a significant difference between two sets of scores. Hence parametric tests are used whenever the characteristics of the data permit. The *robustness* of some parametric tests (e.g. the *t*-test) make it possible to use these techniques even when the assumptions of normality and equal variance have been violated.

4 Independent two-sample tests

The tests described in this chapter deal with the analysis of experiments in which the scores of two independent groups of subjects are to be compared. As suggested in Chapter 1, this design is not particularly sensitive to the effects of the independent variable because subject differences tend to obscure the experimental effects. Nevertheless, much psychological research is based on the independent groups design. This is due partly to its simplicity – one merely divides the subjects into two groups on a random basis – and partly to the lack of any practicable alternative in certain situations, for example, when performance in one condition of an experiment destroys a subject's usefulness in the other.

There are four tests which may be used with this design:

1 Normal distribution (Z) test for independent samples (parametric)
2 t-test for independent samples (parametric)
3 Mann-Whitney test (non-parametric)
4 Chi-square test (non-parametric)

We shall deal with these tests in turn, showing the procedures to be followed and the circumstances under which each test should be used. But before doing this the rationale underlying the first two will be discussed in some detail; this will introduce a number of points which are of general importance.

Rationale of the independent Z and *t*-tests

Choosing the tests

Consider the experiment on traffic noise and reasoning performance. The data for this study were obtained from two independent groups of subjects and should therefore be analysed using one of the four tests listed above. Since parametric tests are more powerful we should consider whether the Z or t-test can be used before looking at the non-parametric alternatives. This means we must decide whether the samples have been drawn from normal populations with equal variance and with measurements on an interval scale (see p. 61). Inspection of the histograms for the two sets of scores (see figure 12) gives us no reason to suppose that the populations are *not* normal – both samples have reasonably symmetrical distributions of the sort one would obtain from a normal population. There appears to be some difference in the variability of the samples, but we have already learned that these tests are robust

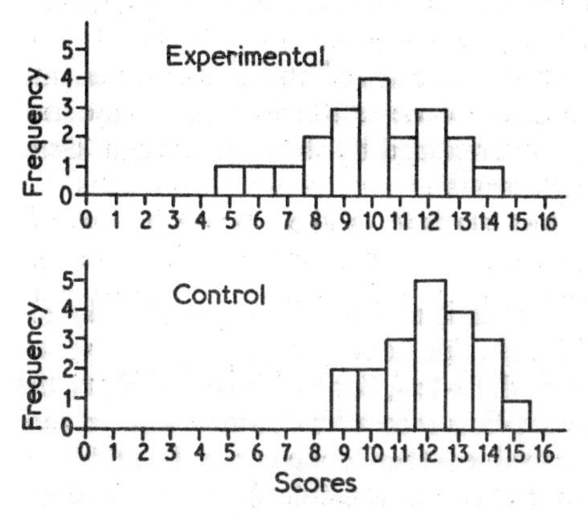

Figure 12 Scores of experimental and control subjects in the traffic noise experiment

enough to cope with modest violations of the equal variance rule, and in this case the difference does not seem very dramatic. (If in doubt, the size of the difference can be assessed statistically; see chapter 7.) Finally, if we assume that each problem on the logical reasoning test is of equal difficulty, then the 'units' of the scale become equal in size, giving us measurement at the interval level. With these assumptions we may now proceed with one of the parametric tests, i.e. either the t-test or the Z test. How we choose between these alternatives will become clear later.

The test statistic

Using the original data from the traffic noise experiment (see p. 25) we find that the control group's mean score was 12.0, whereas the experimental group produced a mean of 9.95. As we learned in the last chapter, the purpose of the statistical test is to discover the probability that this difference arose by chance rather than being caused by the different noise levels. If this probability turns out to be 0.05 or less we shall reject the chance explanation (null hypothesis) and conclude that the traffic noise did have an effect on performance. If the probability exceeds 0.05, the chance explanation cannot be ruled out.

The next step, then, is to calculate p, the probability that the results occurred by chance. In all statistical tests this is done in two stages:

1 The difference between the two sets of scores is converted into a standardized measure of deviation known as the *test statistic*. This stage is performed by the experimenter using the appropriate test formula.
2 The value of the test statistic is then converted into a probability, p, using specially prepared tables.

There is a different test statistic and a different set of tables for each of the tests outlined in this book, but they all involve the same two stages. Thus the t-test, for example, converts the difference between two means into a test statistic known (not surprisingly!) as t. The t value is then looked up in the *t tables* to find the probability that the observed difference arose entirely by chance.

The procedures for doing this are set out on pp. 79–86. That section is completely self-contained, and the reader who simply wishes to analyse some data should turn directly to the computational procedures. However if you are interested in the derivation of the tests themselves – read on!

Derivation of the Z and t-tests

In the previous chapter we saw that it was possible to regard a group of scores as a randomly selected sample from an imaginary population. Under the null (or chance) hypothesis the two groups of scores are samples from the *same* population and they differ because of sampling variability – the tendency for any two samples to vary slightly. On the other hand, the alternate hypothesis states that the two samples come from two different populations, and the sample means differ because the population means differ.

The purpose of a statistical test is to find the probability that the chance hypothesis is true, i.e. the probability that the two samples came from a single population. To find this probability in the traffice noise experiment we need to know how likely it is that two samples drawn from the same population would have means that differed by as much as 2·05 (this is the control mean of 12·0 minus the experimental mean of 9·95). Before we can calculate this probability we need to learn some more about the properties of populations and samples.

WHAT DOES THE DISTRIBUTION OF SAMPLE MEANS LOOK LIKE?

Suppose we drew a very large number of random samples from a population and calculated the mean of each one. If we knew what the distribution of these means looked like, we might be able to work out the probability that any two of them could differ by as much as the two means obtained in our experiment. We shall now perform a mental 'experiment' to discover the properties of this distribution of sample means.

Imagine that you measured the logical reasoning ability of thousands of people, wrote each score on a small piece of paper, and placed all the pieces in a gigantic hat. This could represent our population of scores; it might be normally distributed with a mean of say, 25, and a standard deviation of 10, as shown in figure 13(a). Now suppose that you took a random sample of twenty scores from this population and found the sample mean. This might be, say, 24·6. A second sample might yield a mean of 25·1. And so on. If you worked at this task for long enough you would eventually build up a frequency distribution of the sample means. This would approximate to the smooth curve shown in figure 13(b). This distribution is known as the *sampling distribution of the mean.*

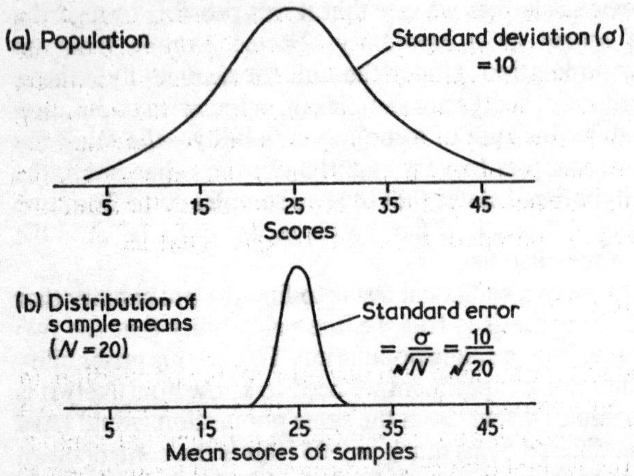

Figure 13 The relationship between a normal population of scores and the distribution of sample means drawn from the population

Note that, like the original population, the sampling distribution is also normal in form. (This is hardly surprising, but actually it can be shown that a sampling distribution tends towards normality as the sample size increases, *irrespective of the shape of the population being sampled.* This is known as the *central limit theorem.*) A second point to note is that the mean of the sampling distribution is the same as the mean of the population. Again this is fairly obvious; although the sample means will vary slightly, we would expect them to average out at the value of the population mean. Finally, note that the variability of the sample means is very much less than the variability among the individual scores in the population. You can see intuitively why this should be so by considering the chance of observing an 'extreme' value. In the original population one might occasionally come across an extremely high or extremely low score. But the chance of obtaining a sample *mean* of this value would be very much smaller, because one would have to select, just by chance, twenty extreme scores in the same sample, and this would be virtually impossible. Rather the tendency is for the high and low scores to cancel each other out in any one sample, so that the sample means will cluster much more closely around the value of the population mean than do the individual scores themselves. Naturally this gravitation towards the mean will depend on the size of the sample, N; the larger the samples, the more tightly clustered the sample means will be around the value of the population mean. This is reflected by the standard deviation of the sampling distribution (known as the *standard error*) which is *less* than the standard deviation of the population. In fact a very simple relationship obtains: the standard error is equal to the standard deviation of the population divided by $\sqrt{N}$. That is:

$$\text{Standard error} = \frac{\sigma}{\sqrt{N}}$$

where σ stands for the standard deviation of the population. (σ is used in preference to s to indicate that we are referring to a feature of the population rather than an individual sample. Similarly the symbol μ is used for the population mean, whereas $\bar{X}$ is used for the sample mean.)

Now that we know about the distribution of the sample means we can return to the question of whether any two particular means are likely to differ by as much as the two means obtained in our experiment. Unfortunately the sampling distribution shown in figure 13(b) does not tell us exactly what we want to know. We could use this distribution to find the probability of obtaining, by chance, a sample mean within some specified range of values, but this is not what is needed here. We wish to know the probability of getting a *difference* between *two* sample means of some particular value. In order to find this we need to consider a slightly different sampling distribution – namely, the sampling distribution for the difference between two means.

THE SAMPLING DISTRIBUTION OF THE DIFFERENCE BETWEEN TWO MEANS

This would be obtained in a similar way to the distribution of a single sample mean. We would again take a large number of random samples from the population, but this time we would select the samples in pairs and calculate the *difference* between the means of each pair of samples. These differences would sometimes be positive and sometimes negative, but the average difference would be zero and the shape of the distribution would be normal. As we are taking *two* means into account when calculating each difference, the variability of the differences will be somewhat greater than the variability of the individual sample means. In fact it can be shown that the standard error of the difference between two means is equal to the standard deviation of the population multiplied by $\sqrt{1/N_1 + 1/N_2}$. That is:

$$\text{Standard error} = \sigma\sqrt{\frac{1}{N_1} + \frac{1}{N_2}}$$

where N_1 and N_2 represent the size of the two samples. (If you are interested in the proof of this relationship, see Goodman, 1962, p. 140). These features of the sampling distribution of the difference between two means are summarized in figure 14.

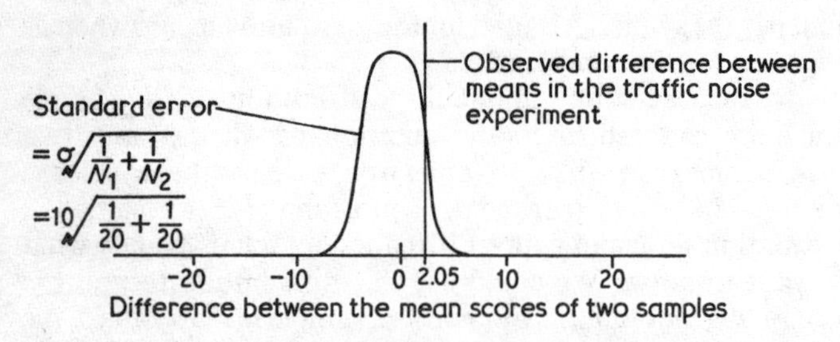

Figure 14 Sampling distribution of the difference between the means of two samples selected from the same population ($N_1 = N_2 = 20$)

We are now well on the way to being able to calculate the probability that the two samples obtained in our experiment could differ by as much as they do, under the assumption that they were both randomly selected from the same population of logical reasoning scores. Figure 14 represents all the possible differences between pairs of means that could be obtained when sampling from a single population. Using our knowledge of the normal distribution (see p. 43) we can find the probability of obtaining a difference as large or larger than any given value. All we need to know is the distance of that difference from the mean value (zero) expressed in units of standard deviation or, in this case, standard error. The difference obtained in the traffic noise experiment was 2·05, and his value has been marked on the sampling distribution of differences in figure 14. The distance between the mean of the sampling distribution and 2·05, expressed in units of standard error, is given by:

$$Z = \frac{2{\cdot}05 - 0}{10\sqrt{\frac{1}{20} + \frac{1}{20}}}$$

Or in general terms using $\bar{X}_1$ and $\bar{X}_2$ to represent the two sample means, the extent to which any difference exceeds zero, measured in units of standard error, is given by:

$$Z = \frac{(\bar{X}_1 - \bar{X}_2) - 0}{\sigma\sqrt{\frac{1}{N_1} + \frac{1}{N_2}}} \qquad (A)$$

Armed with this Z score we may enter table I (p. 172) and find the area of the normal curve which falls above this value. This corresponds to the probability of obtaining a difference as large or larger than $(\bar{X}_1 - \bar{X}_2)$ under the null hypothesis that the two samples were drawn from a single population, i.e. the probability, p, that the difference arose by chance. If p is less than 0·05 then we shall reject the null hypothesis in favour of the alternate hypothesis that the samples were drawn from different populations, i.e. we conclude that there is a real difference between the two samples caused by the change in noise level.

The need for two tests – Z and t

The general formula (A) above is fine so long as we know the value of σ, the standard deviation of the population from which the samples have been drawn. In demonstrating the formula above we just invented a value for σ, namely 10. But we could not do this in a real statistical test; we would need the true value.

Unless some previous research on very large numbers of subjects had established this standard deviation (an unlikely state of affairs) the value of σ would be unknown, and we should have to estimate it from the standard deviations of the scores in the samples themselves. There are two ways this can be done:
(1) *If the samples are reasonably large*, say thirty or more observations, the σ term in formula A is brought inside the square root and simply replaced by the standard deviations of the two samples. The resulting test statistic can still be looked up in the normal distribution (Z) tables and the formula becomes:

$$Z=\frac{(\bar{X}_1-\bar{X}_2)-0}{\sqrt{\dfrac{S_1^{\,2}}{N_1}+\dfrac{S_2^{\,2}}{N_2}}}$$

where S_1 and S_2 are the standard deviations of the two samples whose means are being compared. The zero in the numerator has no effect on the calculation, and is there to remind us that we are comparing the difference in the means with the difference that would be expected if the samples came from the same population, i.e. 0. For practical purposes the formula for a two-sample Z test is therefore:

$$Z=\frac{(\bar{X}_1-\bar{X}_2)}{\sqrt{\dfrac{S_1^{\,2}}{N_1}+\dfrac{S_2^{\,2}}{N_2}}} \qquad (B)$$

The Z statistic is then referred to the normal distribution tables to determine the probability that the samples came from the same population of scores.
(2) *If the samples are small*, say less than thirty observations in each group, the estimate of σ used above is too inaccurate. For small samples it can be shown that the best estimate of the population standard deviation is given by:

$$\hat{\sigma}=\sqrt{\frac{N_1S_1^{\,2}+N_2S_2^{\,2}}{N_1+N_2-2}}$$

where the symbol $\hat{}$ means 'an estimate of'.

When this expression is substituted in formula A the result is a more complicated test statistic which deviates slightly from the normal distribution. This statistic is known as t and is given by:

$$t = \frac{(\bar{X}_1 - \bar{X}_2)\sqrt{(N_1 + N_2 - 2)N_1 N_2}}{\sqrt{(N_1 S_1{}^2 + N_2 S_2{}^2)(N_1 + N_2)}} \qquad (C)$$

As with Z, the value of t is converted into a probability by reference to the appropriate tables (t tables). In this case, however, the sample sizes N_1 and N_2 as well as the t value are needed when looking up the probability (see pp. 83–6).

We can summarize this section on the derivation of Z and t-tests as follows. Under the null hypothesis the two samples of scores have been drawn from a single population. By making certain assumptions about that population we can discover the distribution that would be obtained if many pairs of samples were randomly selected and their means compared. The *observed* difference between the two means obtained in an experiment is then compared with these *expected* differences by using the Z or t formula. If the observed difference is well within the range of differences expected by chance then Z or t will have low values. If the observed difference in means is larger than would normally be obtained by taking two samples from the same population, then the Z or t value will be high. By referring to the appropriate tables the exact probability of the samples coming from the same population can be obtained. If this value is less than 0·05 the samples are said to differ significantly and the alternate hypothesis of a real difference between the mean scores is accepted.

One- and two-tailed tests

The idea of one- and two-tailed tests is important for the understanding of the Z and t-tests, and indeed for all the statistical tests included in this book. The distinction between these two types of test hinges on the nature of the prediction made at the outset of the experiment. If we had predicted the *direction* of the difference between the two conditions (e.g. that noise *impairs* performance relative to no noise) then we have a *one-tailed test*. If, on the other hand, we cannot be so specific (e.g. we predict that noise will have some effect on performance, but we don't know whether it will be positive or negative) then we have a *two-tailed test.*

Now how does this distinction affect the statistical analysis? To answer this question we must consider all the possible results of the experiment. For any given difference between the means there will be a corresponding value of the test statistic. Let us suppose that the appropriate test is a *t*-test. Then we can represent the possible outcomes to the experiment by the distribution of possible *t* values that could have been obtained *if the two samples were drawn from the same population* (the null hypothesis). The most likely result is a *t* of zero – no difference between the means – and the probability falls off on either side of $t = 0$ (see figure 15). The two tails of the distribution represent extreme cases – either $\bar{X}_1$ is much larger than $\bar{X}_2$ (the right-hand tail) or $\bar{X}_2$ is much larger than $\bar{X}_1$ (the left-hand tail). Where on this distribution do we regard the most extreme 5 per cent of the cases to fall? Do we take the most extreme $2\frac{1}{2}$ per cent of the cases at each tail? Or do we take the most extreme 5 per cent of the cases at one tail? Obviously if the test is one-tailed we shall only be interested in extreme cases at one end of the distribution (say the right-hand tail) because we made the specific prediction that $\bar{X}_1$ will be larger than $\bar{X}_2$. Thus we shall consider the results significant if they produce a *t* value in the upper 5 per cent of the distribution (A or more in figure 15). If the test is two-tailed then we shall be interested in extreme cases at *both* ends of the distribution because we predicted a difference between $\bar{X}_1$ and $\bar{X}_2$ in either direction. Thus we shall consider our results significant if they produce a *t* value in the upper $2\frac{1}{2}$ per cent or

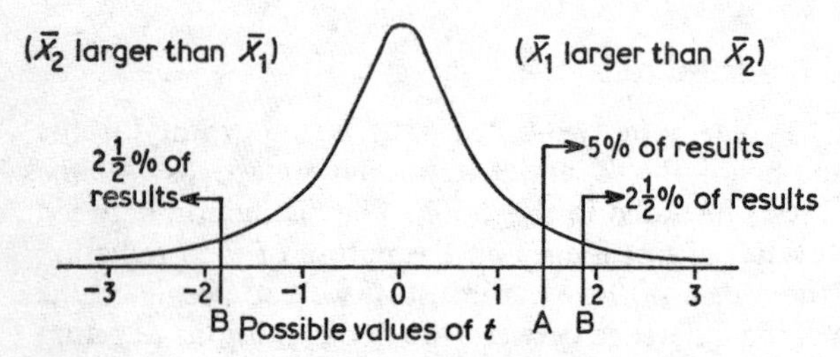

Figure 15 *t* distribution showing the critical values of *t* at the 5 per cent level for a one- and two-tailed test

lower $2\frac{1}{2}$ per cent of the distribution (B or more extreme in figure 15). Thus the critical value of *t* for 5 per cent significance will depend on whether the test is one- or two-tailed. For a one-tailed test we need a less extreme value than for a two-tailed test.

It may be difficult to see why this is so without some further thought. With a one-tailed prediction (or *directional hypothesis*) there is no point in testing results in the 'wrong direction' – e.g. noise *enhancing* performance – but we require a less extreme value of *t* for significance (A in figure 15) if our results are in the predicted direction. With a two-tailed prediction (*non-directional hypothesis*) we shall analyse the data *whichever direction* the difference happens to be in, but we shall require a correspondingly more extreme value of *t* before we accept that the observed difference is significant (B in figure 15). Putting this another way, if we obtain a particular value of *t* from a statistical test, say the value B in figure 15, this will be 5 per cent significant using a two-tailed test, but $2\frac{1}{2}$ per cent significant using a one-tailed test. Obviously it is important that you decide *before* conducting the experiment whether your prediction is directional or non-directional, otherwise you may 'convince yourself' after the experiment that whatever happened was what you predicted.

The normal distribution (Z) test for independent samples

Choice of test

This test is the most powerful device for detecting a difference between the means of two independent samples of scores. A typical application might be a test of whether the mean reaction time of fifty subjects to the onset of a red light is significantly faster than the mean reaction time of fifty *other* subjects to a green light. Since the test is parametric it assumes that the two sets of scores come from normal populations with equal variance, although slight violations of these rules are not critical. It is also assumed that the measurements are on an interval scale.

The above requirements are common to the *Z* and *t*-tests. However the *Z* test also requires large samples – that is, at least thirty subjects in each group – whereas the *t*-test can accommodate smaller samples. These considerations are discussed more fully in the previous section (see pp. 75–6).

Rationale

The Z formula converts the difference between the two sample means into a standardized measure of deviation. Hence the *larger* the value of Z, the more discrepant are the two sets of scores and the *lower* the probability that the differences arose by chance. If this probability falls below 0.05 the chance hypothesis may be rejected in favour of the alternate hypothesis of a real difference between the mean levels of performance in the two conditions. The rationale of the test is described in detail on pp. 73–7.

Z test for independent samples: computation

GENERAL PROCEDURE

I Calculate the two sample means $\bar{X}_1$ and $\bar{X}_2$ using the formula

$$\bar{X} = \frac{\Sigma X}{N} \quad \left(\text{or } \bar{X} = \frac{\Sigma fX}{N} \text{ for grouped data}\right)$$

II Calculate the two sample variances $S_1{}^2$ and $S_2{}^2$ using the formula

$$S^2 = \frac{\Sigma X^2}{N} - \bar{X}^2 \quad \left(\text{or } S^2 = \frac{\Sigma fX^2}{N} - \bar{X}^2 \text{ for grouped data}\right)$$

III Substitute the values of $\bar{X}_1$, $\bar{X}_2$, $S_1{}^2$, $S_2{}^2$, N_1, N_2 in the computational formula for Z

$$Z = \frac{\bar{X}_1 - \bar{X}_2}{\sqrt{\frac{S_1{}^2}{N_1} + \frac{S_2{}^2}{N_2}}}$$

IV Convert Z into a probability that the difference in means arose by chance. Use the normal distribution tables, p. 172. (If the test is two-tailed the probability shown in the tables should be doubled.)

V If the probability of obtaining the difference by chance is *less* than 0·05 (or some other preferred level of significance) then the null hypothesis is rejected and the alternate hypothesis accepted, i.e. the independent variable is presumed to have caused the difference between the sample means.

EXAMPLE

Effect of red and green light signals on reaction time. Experimenter predicts that red signals will produce faster responses than green signals.

Reaction times ($\frac{1}{10}$ s) of subjects responding to red light ($N_1 = 35$)	*Reaction times ($\frac{1}{10}$ s) of subjects responding to green light ($N_2 = 32$)*
5, 4, 5, 5, 6, 4, 7, 6, 5, 6, 6, 5, 5, 5, 6, 8, 4, 6, 5, 7, 7, 5, 5, 6, 5, 6, 5, 6, 8, 6, 5, 6, 7, 5, 4	6, 7, 6, 5, 6, 7, 7, 7, 6, 5, 6, 8, 6, 7, 8, 6, 5, 7, 6, 8, 9, 6, 7, 5, 5, 6, 7, 7, 6, 5, 8, 6

I
$$\bar{X}_1 = \frac{\Sigma X_1}{N_1} = \frac{5+4+5\ldots+5+4}{35} = \frac{196}{35} = 5{\cdot}600$$

$$\bar{X}_2 = \frac{\Sigma X_2}{N_2} = \frac{6+7+6\ldots+8+6}{32} = \frac{206}{32} = 6{\cdot}438$$

II
$$S_1{}^2 = \frac{\Sigma X_1{}^2}{N_1} - \bar{X}_1{}^2 = \frac{5^2+4^2\ldots5^2+4^2}{35} - 5{\cdot}6^2 = \frac{1134}{35} - 31{\cdot}360 = 1{\cdot}040$$

$$S_2{}^2 = \frac{\Sigma X_2{}^2}{N_2} - \bar{X}_2{}^2 = \frac{6^2+7^2\ldots8^2+6^2}{32} - 6{\cdot}438^2 = \frac{1360}{32} - 41{\cdot}448 = 1{\cdot}052$$

III
$$Z = \frac{(\bar{X}_1 - \bar{X}_2)}{\sqrt{\frac{S_1{}^2}{N_1} + \frac{S_2{}^2}{N_2}}} = \frac{(5{\cdot}6 - 6{\cdot}438)}{\sqrt{\frac{1{\cdot}04}{35} + \frac{1{\cdot}052}{32}}}$$

$$= \frac{-0{\cdot}838}{\sqrt{0{\cdot}626}} = \frac{-0{\cdot}838}{0{\cdot}25}$$

$$= -3{\cdot}352$$

IV The negative value of Z is of no particular significance: it arises from the fact that $\bar{X}_2$ is larger than $\bar{X}_1$. Had the samples been set out in the reverse order Z would have been positive, and we can therefore ignore the minus sign.

Using table I: A Z value of 3·35 corresponds to a probability smaller than 0·0005. (As the test is one-tailed, this probability level is *not* adjusted.)

V *Conclusion.* The probability that these two samples could have been randomly selected from the same population is very low,* and we can therefore reject the null hypothesis at the 0·05 level of significance. We conclude that the difference between the two sets of reaction times did not arise by chance but was produced by the difference in the colours of the light signals.

The *t*-test for independent samples

Choice of test

This is a parametric test of the difference between the means of two independent samples. It might be used, for example, to determine whether a random sample of ten patients treated with drug A recovered more rapidly from an infection than another sample of twelve patients treated with drug B. Like the Z test, the *t*-test assumes that the two sets of scores come from normal populations with equal variance, but the test is not affected by minor violations of these rules. It is also assumed that the measurements are on an interval scale.

Although both the Z and *t*-tests are parametric two-sample tests, the *t*-test is specially adapted for small samples (where one or both samples are smaller than thirty) and is somewhat less powerful than the Z test. Further details are given on pp. 75–6.

* Note that this probability is much lower than the critical value of 0·05 (or 5 per cent) which is normally required for significance. The result obtained here is therefore very highly significant and we can be very confident that the observed difference is a reliable one.

Rationale

In essence the t formula measures the size of the difference between the means of two samples and converts this into a standard measure of deviation. Hence a *large* value of t signifies a marked difference between the sample means and, correspondingly, a *low* probability that the samples vary purely by chance. If this probability falls below 0·05 the chance hypothesis may be rejected in favour of the alternate hypothesis that there is a genuine and reliable difference between the levels of performance in the two experimental conditions. The rationale of the test is described more fully on pp. 69–77.

Degrees of freedom

Unlike the Z test, the t statistic cannot be converted into a probability without taking account of the sample sizes, or more precisely the degrees of freedom of the test. Before dealing with the computational procedure we therefore define this term.

Suppose we calculate the standard deviation of a set of N scores. How many of those scores are actually free to vary and to contribute to the value of S? There is a sense in which only $N-1$ of the scores are free to vary. The reason for this is that we use the value of the mean in computing the value of S. Once the mean is fixed for N numbers, only $N-1$ of them are free to take any value – the value of the Nth score must be such as to give the whole set the predetermined mean. So when we calculate S_1 and S_2 in the t-test, the number of observations that are truly free to vary are (N_1-1) plus (N_2-1) or (N_1+N_2-2). Now the shape of the t distribution depends directly on the number of freely varying scores that were used in the calculation of S_1 and S_2. Consequently, when we come to interpret t in terms of a probability (p), we need to find the p value that is appropriate for (N_1+N_2-2) degrees of freedom or *df*. This requirement is embodied in the computational formula by writing the number of degrees of freedom as a subscript to t.

t-test for independent samples: computation

GENERAL PROCEDURE

I Calculate the two samples means $\bar{X}_1$ and $\bar{X}_2$ using the formula:

$$\bar{X} = \frac{\Sigma X}{N}$$

II Calculate the two sample variances $S_1{}^2$ and $S_2{}^2$ using the formula:

$$S^2 = \frac{\Sigma X^2}{N} - \bar{X}^2$$

III Substitute the values of $\bar{X}_1$, $\bar{X}_2$, $S_1{}^2$, $S_2{}^2$, N_1, N_2 in the computational formula for t:

$$t_{N_1+N_2-2} = \frac{(\bar{X}_1 - \bar{X}_2)\sqrt{(N_1+N_2-2)N_1N_2}}{\sqrt{(N_1S_1{}^2+N_2S_2{}^2)(N_1+N_2)}}$$

IV Find the number of degrees of freedom using the formula:

$$df = N_1 + N_2 - 2.$$

V Find the value of t needed for your chosen level of significance using table II, p. 174. This critical value will depend on (1) the number of degrees of freedom, and (2) whether the prediction is directional or not.

VI If the observed value of t is *equal* to or *greater* than the critical value of t, reject the null hypothesis in favour of the alternate hypothesis, i.e. conclude that the independent variable had an effect on behaviour.

EXAMPLE

Effects of two drugs on a perceptual–motor skill. Experimenter predicts that Drug *1* will produce higher scores than Drug 2.

Group receiving Drug 1 ($N_1=5$)		*Group receiving Drug 2* ($N_2=7$)	
X_1	X_1^2	X_2	X_2^2
6	36	4	16
8	64	7	49
7	49	5	25
9	81	4	16
8	64	5	25
		6	36
		4	16
$\Sigma X_1=38$	$\Sigma X_1^2=294$	$\Sigma X_2=35$	$\Sigma X_2^2=183$

I $\bar{X}_1=\dfrac{\Sigma X_1}{N_1}=\dfrac{38}{5}=7{\cdot}6$ $\qquad$ $\bar{X}_2=\dfrac{\Sigma X_2}{N_2}=\dfrac{35}{7}=5{\cdot}0$

II $S_1^2=\dfrac{\Sigma X_1^2}{N_1}-\bar{X}_1^2$ $\qquad$ $S_2^2=\dfrac{\Sigma X_2^2}{N_2}-\bar{X}_2^2$

$=\dfrac{294}{5}-7{\cdot}6^2$ $\qquad$ $=\dfrac{183}{7}-5^2$

$=1{\cdot}04$ $\qquad$ $=1{\cdot}143$

III $$t_{N_1+N_2-2}=\frac{(\bar{X}_1-\bar{X}_2)\sqrt{(N_1+N_2-2)N_1N_2}}{\sqrt{(N_1S_1^2+N_2S_2^2)(N_1+N_2)}}$$

$$=\frac{(7{\cdot}6-5{\cdot}0)\sqrt{(5+7-2)5\times 7}}{\sqrt{(5\times 1{\cdot}04+7\times 1{\cdot}143)(5+7)}}$$

$$=\frac{2{\cdot}6\sqrt{10\times 5\times 7}}{\sqrt{13{\cdot}201\times 12}}=3{\cdot}86$$

IV $df=5+7-2=10$

V Using table II: For ten degrees of freedom the value of t required for the 5 per cent level of significance (one-tailed) is 1·812.

VI *Conclusion.* As the observed t is greater than 1·812 it is unlikely* that our results could have arisen by chance. We may therefore accept the alternate hypothesis that Drug *1* produces higher performance than Drug *2*.

The Mann-Whitney test

Choice of the test

This test is frequently used as an alternative to the t-test for independent samples. It has very similar functions, but can be used with data that are measured on an ordinal scale, and the test makes no assumptions about the shape of population distributions. Even when it is used with data that are appropriate to the t-test, its power to detect significance is not very much less than that of the t-test itself. Hence this technique is extremely useful.

A typical application of the test might involve the comparison of two independent groups of subjects who were taught to read by different methods and subsequently rated on a scale of reading 'fluency' from 1 to 10. It is unlikely that such measurements would possess interval scaling, since there is nothing approximating to a 'unit' of fluency. Hence the t-test would not be strictly appropriate. However, the ratings would almost certainly achieve ordinal scaling; that is, they could be used to *rank* individuals in order of fluency. Hence the Mann-Whitney test could be applied to the data. Once ordinal scaling is assumed it is no longer sensible to calculate the mean of a set of ratings. For this reason the Mann-Whitney test cannot be used to decide whether two groups of scores differ specifically in their *means*, and in this respect it is not perfectly analogous to the t-test. However, the Mann-Whitney does allow us to test the more general hypothesis that one set of scores tends to be higher (or lower) than another set. This is perfectly adequate for most psychological predictions.

* To be precise, the probability that the difference between the means arose by chance is less than 0·05.

Rationale

Like most non-parametric tests the rationale behind the Mann-Whitney test is extremely simple. Imagine two samples of scores drawn from the same population. If we combine these samples into one larger group and then rank the scores from lowest to highest we would expect to find the scores from both original samples randomly arranged in the combined ranking. If, however, most of the scores from one sample were lower in rank than most of the scores from the other sample, we should begin to suspect that the two samples were not drawn from the same underlying population. By finding the sum of the ranks of one of the samples, the Mann-Whitney test allows us to determine the probability that a given separation between the ranks of the two samples could have arisen by chance. If this probability is very low (i.e. $\leqslant 0{\cdot}05$) we may reject the null hypothesis that the ordering of ranks is purely random, in favour of the alternate hypothesis that the independent variable has produced a difference in the levels of performance of the two groups. As with the *t*-test a given difference between the two sets of rankings is regarded as more significant if the direction of the difference was predicted before the experiment (one-tailed test), than if it was not (two-tailed test).

The Mann-Whitney test: computation

GENERAL PROCEDURE

I Let N_1 be the size of the smaller group of scores and N_2 the size of the larger group.

II Rank the combined set of $N_1 + N_2$ scores from the lowest to highest value. Use rank 1 for the lowest, 2 for the next lowest, and so on.

III Find the sum of the ranks for the smaller group and call this R_1.

IV Substitute the values of N_1, N_2 and R_1 in the following formula and calculate U:

$$U = N_1 N_2 + \frac{N_1(N_1+1)}{2} - R_1$$

V Substitute the values of U, N_1 and N_2 in the following formula and calculate U':

$$U' = N_1 N_2 - U$$

VI Find the critical value of U needed for significance at the desired level using table VI (p. 177). The critical value will depend on (1) the values of N_1 and N_2, and (2) whether or not the prediction was directional.

VII If the observed value of U or U' (whichever is the smaller) is *less* than or equal to the critical value of U, reject the null hypothesis.

TIES

If two or more scores have the same value we give each score the average of the ranks that would have been used if there was not a tie. Thus if two scores would have occupied rank positions 6 and 7, but are equal, they both receive the rank of $6\frac{1}{2}$. But note that these two scores have 'used up' *two* ranks, 6 and 7, so that the next highest score will receive rank 8.

The presence of ties tends to lower the chance of obtaining a significant result, but this effect is very slight. For large numbers of ties, or when the results are on the borderline of significance, it may be worthwhile applying a correction for ties to the formula. The details are given in Siegel (1956).

EXAMPLE

Ratings of fluency for children taught to read by two different methods. Experimenter predicts that there will be a difference between the effectiveness of Methods A and B.

Ratings of group taught by Method A ($N_1=6$)	*Ranks*	*Ratings of group taught by Method B* ($N_2=8$)	*Ranks*
5	$6\frac{1}{2}$	4	5
7	$10\frac{1}{2}$	6	$8\frac{1}{2}$
7	$10\frac{1}{2}$	3	4
6	$8\frac{1}{2}$	5	$6\frac{1}{2}$
9	13	2	$2\frac{1}{2}$
10	14	1	1
		2	$2\frac{1}{2}$
	$R_1=63$	8	12

IV $U=N_1N_2+\dfrac{N_1(N_1+1)}{2}-R_1$

$$U = 6\times 8+\frac{6\times 7}{2}-63 = 6$$

V $U' = N_1N_2-U = 6\times 8-6 = 42$

VI Using table VI: For $N_1=6$, $N_2=8$, the critical value of U for 5 per cent significance (two-tailed) is 8.

VII *Conclusion.* As the (smaller) observed U is *less* than the critical value of U for 5 per cent significance, we can conclude that there is a significant difference between the two groups: the effects of the two teaching methods are different.

LARGE SAMPLES: N_2 LARGER THAN 20

Table VI does not give critical values for U when N_2 is larger than 20. When this occurs it is possible to approximate U to a Z score, and to use the normal distribution table (table I, p. 173) to find the significance of the results. In order to find the appropriate value of Z we substitute in the following formula:

$$Z = \frac{U - \dfrac{N_1 N_2}{2}}{\sqrt{\dfrac{N_1 N_2 (N_1 + N_2 + 1)}{12}}}$$

Suppose, for example, we obtained a U value of 264 after completing step IV in the general procedure. If N_1 was 16 and N_2 was 24 the Z score would be:

$$\frac{264 - \dfrac{16 \times 24}{2}}{\sqrt{\dfrac{16 \times 24 \times 41}{12}}} = 1{\cdot}988$$

We can now look up Z in table I to find the probability that the observed difference between the rankings could have occurred by chance. This probability is 0·0233, indicating a significant difference between the two groups. (Note that table I gives one-tailed probabilities; if the experimenter's prediction was non-directional, it would be necessary to double the p value before stating the significance of the results.)

The chi-square (χ^2) test for independent samples

Choice of the test

So far we have considered two sample tests which can be used to compare the scores of two groups on various types of quantitative variable – logical reasoning scores, fluency ratings, and so forth. Quite often, however, we are interested in some non-quantitative aspect of a subject's behaviour, for example, does a subject 'think aloud' or not? Does he consciously use mnemonics in a memory experiment, or doesn't he? Does he maintain eye contact with an interviewer, or does he look away? These measurements, in so far as they are measurements at all, are said to constitute *nominal scaling* (see p. 62). It is readily apparent that we cannot compare two groups with regard to their *average* performance on such variables – what is the 'average' score of two subjects, of whom one thinks aloud and one doesn't? All we can say is whether the groups differ in the *proportion* of subjects who come into one category rather than another. Thus we might predict that subjects who are tested by members of their own sex in a problem solving task would be more likely to think aloud than subjects who are tested by members of the opposite sex. To test this prediction we would record the *frequency* of occasions on which subjects in each group did or did not think aloud and then compare the *relative frequency* of thinking aloud across the two groups of subjects.

Whenever our data consist of frequency counts of the number of times different events occur, the χ^2 test can be used to compare the proportions of these events in two independent samples. Even if the data are truly quantitative – e.g. reaction times under two levels of stress – there is nothing to stop us converting these scores into frequencies. For example, we could choose some arbitrary value of reaction time, and categorize subjects as fast or slow according to whether their performance was above or below this value. We could then conduct a χ^2 test to see if the proportion of fast subjects was any higher under one level of stress than another. This approach is perfectly legitimate, but it does, of course, waste most of the information in the original data, and our chance of detecting a significant result is accordingly reduced.

Rationale

Suppose we test thirty subjects using the 'same sex' experimenter (i.e. a male experimenter for a male subject, female experimenter for female subject), and twenty-seven subjects using the 'opposite sex' experimenter. We assume, of course, that subjects have been allocated to the two conditions at random, and we record the number of subjects who were observed to 'think aloud' in both groups. We can present the results in the form of a 2×2 contingency table, as illustrated in table 10. Our task, as with all statistical tests, is to compute the probability that the difference between the two groups could have arisen purely by chance. The approach used in the χ^2 test is to compute the frequencies that *would have* occurred if the two groups were identical with respect to the proportion of people

Table 10 Imaginary results of an experiment on the proportion of people who think aloud under different circumstances (table shows frequencies)

	Same sex experimenter	*Different sex experimenter*	*(Marginal frequencies)*
Thought aloud	20	9	29
Didn't think aloud	10	18	28
Marginal frequencies	30	27	57

who think aloud (these are the *expected* frequencies). The χ^2 value is then calculated on the basis of the *difference* between the expected frequencies (E values) and the observed frequencies (O values). The statistical tables then tell us the probability that a difference as large or larger than that represented by χ^2 could have occurred by chance.

The only difficulty here is in establishing the value of the expected frequencies under the hypothesis that the two groups are identical with respect to the dependent variable. To find the expected frequency for the top, left-hand cell of the contingency table, we reason as follows:

1 Overall, 29/57 of the total group of subjects think aloud (this is obtained from the *marginal* frequencies shown in the table).
2 There were thirty subjects in the 'same sex' condition.
3 Therefore, if there was no difference between the groups 29/57 of the thirty subjects should have thought aloud: i.e. $29/57 \times 30 (= 15{\cdot}26)$.

The same procedure can be used to find the remaining expected frequencies. In general, then, the E value for any cell is given by:

$$E = \frac{\text{Row total} \times \text{Column total}}{\text{Grand total}}$$

But note that we could obtain the expected frequencies for all the other cells by subtraction, since the expected frequencies must add up to the marginal totals. This demonstrates quite graphically that there is only one degree of freedom in a 2×2 χ^2 test. The assumptions needed to do the test mean that only one value is really free to vary. Since χ^2 is one of those statistics whose significance depends on *df*, we need to note this point.

Having obtained the expected frequencies we can now compute the difference between these and the observed values. χ^2 is not based on the simple quantity $\Sigma(O-E)$, but on a slightly more complex measure of the difference between O and E, thus:

$$\chi^2 = \sum \frac{(O-E)^2}{E}$$

In words, we are required to square the difference between each observation and its expected value, divide this square by the expected value, and *then* add together the different values of $(O-E)^2/E$ corresponding to the four cells.

The above formula 'assumes' that the quantity O can take on any value – that it is *continuous*. But, in point of fact, we know that O can only take on integral values – 3, 4, 5, etc. – and not values that fall between whole numbers (we can't observe half a person!). In order to correct for this lack of continuity we should adjust the above formula, as follows:

$$\chi^2 = \sum \frac{(|O-E|-\frac{1}{2})^2}{E}$$

Note that we now take the *absolute* value of $(O-E)$, whether this is positive or negative, and subtract $\frac{1}{2}$ from it, before squaring. This correction, known as *Yates's correction*, is incorporated in the computational formula given in the next section. When the sample size is very small the value of χ^2 cannot be meaningfully interpreted, even after Yates's correction has been made, and it is necessary to use another test which gives an exact measure of the probabilities of various outcomes (see Siegel, 1956, or Edgington, 1969). As a rough guide χ^2 should not be used when one or more of the *expected* frequencies falls below five.

GENERAL PROCEDURE

(Note. The rationale of the test can best be seen from the formulae given in the previous section. However, a more convenient 'computational formula' has been devised, and this will be used here.)

I Let the values of the cell frequencies be represented as follows:

A	B	A+B
C	D	C+D
A+C	B+D	N

II Substitute the values of A, B, C, D and N in the following formula, and calculate χ^2:

$$\chi^2 = \frac{N(|AD - BC| - \frac{1}{2}N)^2}{(A+B)(C+D)(A+C)(B+D)}$$

(Note that the quantity $|AD-BC|$ is taken as positive even if BC is larger than AD.)

III Find the critical value of χ^2 needed for significance at the desired level using table III (p. 175). The critical value will depend on (1) the degrees of freedom (=1), and (2) whether the *direction* of the difference in proportions was predicted in advance of the experiment.

IV If the observed value of χ^2 is greater than or equal to the critical value the difference between the proportions in the two groups is significant.

EXAMPLE

Effect of the experimenter on the subjects' enjoyment of a task. The prediction is that a higher proportion of subjects will enjoy a task conducted by Experimenter 1 rather than by Experimenter 2.

	Subjects tested by Experimenter 1	*Subjects tested by Experimenter 2*	
Enjoyed	15	10	25
Not enjoyed	10	12	22
	25	22	47

I $A = 15, B = 10, C = 10, D = 12, N = 47$

II $$\chi^2 = \frac{N(|AD - BC| - \frac{1}{2}N)^2}{(A+B)(C+D)(A+C)(B+D)}$$

$$= \frac{47(|15 \times 12 - 10 \times 10| - \frac{1}{2} \times 47)^2}{25 . 22 . 25 . 22} = 0{\cdot}496$$

III Using table III: for one degree of freedom the value of χ^2 required for the 5 per cent level of significance (one-tailed) is 2·71.

IV *Conclusion.* As the observed χ^2 is *less* than 2·71 there is no significant evidence for the prediction that Experimenter 1 is more likely to induce enjoyment in his subjects than Experimenter 2. We cannot reject the null hypothesis. (Note that we do not speak of *accepting* the null hypothesis; since our results are not significant we cannot confidently reject the null hypothesis, but we have certainly not *proved* it correct.)

One final point needs to be made concerning the interpretation of the p value obtained from the χ^2 statistics. Since χ^2 measures the *discrepancy* between actual results and those expected by chance, it takes only positive values. The probability associated with a particular value of χ^2 therefore tells us the chance of a given difference arising, *whatever the direction of the difference between the two groups.* Hence the probability values are *two-tailed.* If we are able to predict which of two proportions will be larger we must divide the p value associated with our χ^2 by two, to get the one-tailed probability. (Note: don't be confused into thinking that because we are only interested in high values of χ^2 we must be using a one-tailed test; these high values represent differences in *both* directions, so the probabilities associated with them are *two-tailed.*)

The above distinction between one- and two-tailed interpretations of χ^2 *only* makes sense in a 2×2 contingency table. It is, however, possible to extend χ^2 to more elaborate designs – say where there are three groups and the dependent variable takes one of four discrete values (e.g. Labour, Conservative, Liberal, other). In these cases we cannot talk about the *direction* of a difference and the question of one- and two-tailed tests does not arise.

Non-experimental uses of the χ^2 test

The example given in the previous section involved the manipulation of an independent variable (the experimenter) and the observation of its *effect* on a dependent variable (enjoyment); this is a genuine experiment in the sense defined in Chapter 1. However, χ^2 is used more frequently in psychology to look at *correlations* or associations between *naturally* occurring changes in two or more factors. For example, we might be interested in the relationship between personality type (introvert or extrovert) and employment record (frequent or infrequent job changes). We could not manipulate either of these variables directly, but we could certainly classify a group of subjects on both variables, and place the results in a 2×2 contingency table in the normal way. These data could then be analysed by the χ^2 test in the manner described in previous sections. Although the procedure would be identical, the interpretation of a significant result would be somewhat different. Significance would represent a stronger than chance relationship between the two variables, but it would not imply any *causal* connection between them, as is the case in an experiment. A correlation coefficient, which measures the strength of the relationship between two variables (see chapter 8) can be derived from a 2×2 table (see Chambers, 1982.)

When χ^2 is used to search for associations between variables, it is often used to analyse tables with more than two rows and columns. For example, we may be interested in the relationship between social class (upper/middle/lower) and drinking habits (frequent/occasional/never). This would constitute a 3×3 contingency table. In order to test for relationships between variables in such tables one calculates χ^2 from the basic formula *without* using Yates's correction, i.e.:

$$\chi^2 = \sum \frac{(O - E)^2}{E}$$

The values of E can still be found from the formula:

$$E = \frac{\text{Row total} \times \text{Column total}}{\text{Grand total}}$$

When looking up χ^2 for these more elaborate tables it is necessary to calculate the degrees of freedom from the formula: $df = (\text{number of rows} - 1)(\text{number of columns} - 1)$. In all other respects the normal procedures apply (see pp. 91–4).

Chapter summary

The tests described in this chapter apply to the analysis of differences between two independent samples of scores. Of the four tests covered, the Z and t-tests are the most powerful – that is, the most likely to detect significance when it is present in the data. However, these tests depend on assumptions which are often violated by psychological data – i.e. normality, homogeneity of variance and interval scaling. It is therefore better, on occasions, to use the non-parametric equivalent of these tests, the Mann-Whitney, which is almost as powerful as the t-test. The Mann-Whitney makes no assumptions about the populations from which the samples have been drawn, and can be used

5

Related two-sample tests

In chapter 4 we were interested in comparing two independent groups of subjects on some variable of interest. If a difference was obtained we wished to show that this was probably caused by the independent variable, and not by chance differences in the abilities or motivations of the members of the two groups. In practice this task is a difficult one, because subjects tend to vary so dramatically on some variables that we require very large groups before we can expect the group differences to balance out and allow us to draw inferences about the experimental manipulations. The related samples designs come to our aid in this dilemma by providing us with pairs of observations that come from closely matched subjects tested under the two conditions of the experiment. Statistical analysis of the difference score for each pair is thus more sensitive to the effects of the independent variable than the gross comparisons of highly variable groups of scores. Thus, *when they are appropriate* (see p. 16), related group designs are much to be preferred over the independent groups design.

In this chapter, then, we are concerned with tests appropriate to data coming from related samples – that is, designs in which individual subjects are matched in some way across the two conditions of the experiment. This may be done using a *repeated measures* design in which each subject performs in *both* conditions of the experiment. Alternatively, pairs of individuals may be selected on the basis of possessing very similar ratings on one or more characteristics. This is the *matched subjects* design. Both designs are treated identically as far as statistical testing is concerned.

We shall now consider the three tests for comparing related samples:

The *t*-test for related samples
The Wilcoxon test
The sign test

The t-test for related samples

Choice of the test

The *t*-test is the most powerful of the related sample tests and should be considered first. The assumptions underlying this test are: (1) that the difference scores (one for each pair of observations) may be regarded as a random sample of differences from a normal population; and (2) that the measurements are on an interval scale. We have already mentioned the robustness of the *t*-test with respect to violations of these assumptions, and the same latitude applies here. Provided that the sample of differences obtained in an experiment does not suggest glaring deviations from normality in the population, and that the measurement of the dependent variable approximates to interval scaling, the *t*-test may be used.

Rationale

Suppose we wish to compare the effects of two drugs on the drinking behaviour of rats. We have ten rats available, and it is decided to test each rat under *both* drugs, i.e. a repeated measures design is used (of course, we must take care to separate the two tests in time so that no interactions between the effects of the drugs are possible). Having completed the experiment we shall have a list of ten pairs of scores (call then X_1s and X_2s) representing, say, the amounts drunk in the 30 minutes following the administration of each drug.

Now let us consider the values of the difference scores for each pair of observations. Call these differences d, where $d = X_1 - X_2$. If two drugs are having equal effects on behaviour (null hypothesis), then the average value of d ($\bar{d}$) should be about zero; that is, by chance alone X_1 will exceed X_2 about as often as X_2 will exceed X_1. If, however, one drug is having more effect than the other (alternate hypothesis), then we should get a substantial value of $\bar{d}$ – either negative or positive depending on which drug is the more effective. Now in the t-test the observed ds are regarded as a random sample from a normal population of ds. Under the null hypothesis this population has a mean value of zero and any deviation from zero in the sample mean, $\bar{d}$ is assumed to reflect sampling variability. Under the alternate hypothesis the non-zero value of $\bar{d}$ is, of course, ascribed to a real difference between the effects of the two drugs, equivalent to postulating a non-zero mean in the population of differences. In order to decide between these alternatives, we proceed as usual to calculate the probability of obtaining our results under the null hypothesis. At this point we can forget that the ds represent differences, and simply regard them as the raw data. The question then is: what is the probability of getting a sample of observations (ds) with a mean as large or larger than $\bar{d}$, from a population in which the mean is zero? Using the notion of the sampling distribution of the mean (see p. 71) it can be shown that this probability corresponds to a t value, thus:

$$t_{N-1} = \frac{\text{Difference between sample and population means}}{\text{Standard error of the mean}}$$

$$= \frac{\bar{d} - 0}{S_d / \sqrt{N-1}}$$

where N is the sample size (number of ds) and s_d is the standard deviation of the ds, and $N-1$ is the number of degrees of freedom.

t-test for related samples: computation

GENERAL PROCEDURE

I Calculate the difference, d, between each pair of scores: $(X_1 - X_2)$. Subtract consistently and be sure to record the minus signs.

II Calculate the mean difference using:

$$\bar{d} = \frac{\Sigma d}{N}$$

III Calculate the standard deviation of the differences using the formula:

$$S_d = \sqrt{\frac{\Sigma d^2}{N} - \bar{d}^2}$$

IV Substitute the values of the mean difference ($\bar{d}$), the standard deviation of the differences (S_d), and the sample size (N) in the following formula and calculate t:

$$t_{N-1} = \frac{\bar{d}}{S_d / \sqrt{N-1}}$$

V Find the critical value of t for the desired level of significance using table II, p. 174. This value will depend on (1) the number of degrees of freedom ($N-1$ in this test) and (2) whether the *direction* of the difference between the two conditions was predicted before the experiment.

VI If the observed value of t is equal to or greater than the critical value, reject the null hypothesis in favour of the alternate hypothesis – i.e. conclude that the independent variable has had an effect on behaviour.

EXAMPLE

Effect of drugs on drinking behaviour in rats. The experimenter predicts a difference between the effects of Drug I and Drug II.

Rat	*Amount drunk under Drug I (cc)* X_1	*Amount drunk under Drug II (cc)* X_2	*Differences* (X_1-X_2) d	*Differences squared* d^2
1	4	6	−2	4
2	7	8	−1	1
3	5	4	1	1
4	4	8	−4	16
5	9	8	1	1
6	7	10	−3	9
7	6	8	−2	4
8	7	7	0	0
9	5	9	−4	16
10	7	9	−2	4
			$\Sigma d = -16$	$\Sigma d^2 = 56$

II $\bar{d} = \frac{\Sigma d}{N} = \frac{-16}{10} = -1{\cdot}6$

III $S_d = \sqrt{\frac{\Sigma d^2}{N} - \bar{d}^2} = \sqrt{\frac{56}{10} - (-1{\cdot}6)^2} = \sqrt{5{\cdot}6 - 2{\cdot}56}$

$= 1{\cdot}7436$

IV $t_{N-1} = \frac{\bar{d}}{S_d/\sqrt{N-1}} = \frac{-1{\cdot}6}{1{\cdot}7436/\sqrt{9}} = \frac{-1{\cdot}6 \times 3}{1{\cdot}7436} = -2{\cdot}75$*

V Using table II: For nine degrees of freedom the value of t required for the 5 per cent significance (two-tailed) is 2·262.

VI *Conclusion.* As the observed value of t is greater than 2·262, we can conclude that there is a significant difference between the effects of the drugs on drinking behaviour.

*The *negative* value of t is of no particular significance. If we had defined the difference as $X_2 - X_1$ instead of $X_1 - X_2$, the t value would have come out positive. The t value is treated as positive when it is compared with the critical value required for significance.

The Wilcoxon test

Choice of the test

The Wilcoxon matched-pairs signed-ranks test is the non-parametric equivalent of the t-test for related samples. Although the Wilcoxon makes no assumptions about population distributions it is nevertheless almost as powerful as the t-test in situations where both tests could be used.

The only requirement for this test is that it should be possible for us to rank the difference scores; that is, to make the judgement that one pair of scores differs more (or less) than another pair. The level of measurement implied by this is almost that of interval scaling, that is measurement in units. Since the t-test also requires interval measurement, the main justification for using the Wilcoxon in preference to t is to avoid the normality assumption, and, at a more mundane level, to save time.

Wilcoxon test: computation

GENERAL PROCEDURE

I Calculate the difference, d, between each pair of scores: $(X_1 - X_2)$. Subtract consistently and be sure to record the minus signs.

II Rank the differences in order from the smallest (rank 1) to the largest (rank N). Ignore the sign of the differences when ranking their magnitude.*

III Add together the ranks corresponding to the differences with the *less* frequent sign. Call this T.

IV Find the critical value of T needed for significance at the desired level using table V, p. 176. The critical value will depend on (1) the size of the sample (i.e. the number of pairs, N), and (2) whether the *direction* of the difference between conditions was predicted before the experiment.

V If the observed value of T is *less* than or equal to the critical value, reject the null hypothesis in favour of the alternate hypothesis.

* *Ties*. There are two sorts of ties that can occur in this test: (1) the two *scores* in a pair may be tied, in which case $d = 0$, and (2) two (or more) ds may be tied. If a pair of scores is tied, the pair is dropped from the analysis, and the value of N is reduced accordingly. If two or more ds are tied, each one is given the average of the ranks that would otherwise have been used (see p. 88).

Rationale

Consider the set of difference scores. Some differences will be positive, some negative. Some differences will be large, others small. If the experimental conditions are equivalent we should expect about the same number of negative as positive differences, and we should expect the sizes of the negative differences to be about the same as the sizes of the positive differences. On the other hand, if there is a significant effect, we should expect to find many, large, positive differences and only a few, smaller, negative differences (or vice versa, depending on the way the subtraction was done). Thus if we rank the differences according to their size, and find the sum of the ranks of the differences with the less frequent signs, we shall have a statistic which has *low* values when there is a significant effect in the data. This statistic can then be compared with the critical 'low' value which should only occur 5 per cent of the time by chance.

EXAMPLE
Effect of drugs on drinking behaviour in rats. The experimenter predicts a difference between the effects of Drug I and Drug II.

Rat	*Amount drunk Drug I (cc)* X_1	*Amount drunk Drug II (cc)* X_2	*Differences* (X_1-X_2) d	*Ranked differences*
1	4	6	−2	5
2	7	8	−1	2
3	5	4	1	2
4	4	8	−4	8½
5	9	8	1	2
6	7	10	−3	7
7	6	8	−2	5
8	7	7	0	(omitted)
9	5	9	−4	8½
10	7	9	−2	5

III T=Sum of ranks of differences with less frequent sign
$=2+2=4$
(In this example the positive differences are the less frequent.)

IV Using table V: For $N=9$ (one pair discarded) the critical value of T for 5 per cent significance (two-tailed) is 6.

V *Conclusion.* As the observed value of T is less than 6, we can conclude that there is a significant difference between the effects of the drugs on drinking behaviour.

LARGE SAMPLES: N LARGER THAN 25

Table V only gives critical values of T for 25 or fewer pairs. When N is larger than 25 the distribution of T is almost exactly normal with a mean of $[N(N+1)]/4$ and a standard deviation of:

$$\sqrt{\frac{N(N+1)(2N+1)}{24}}$$

Thus the probability of getting a T as small or smaller than the observed value, under the null hypothesis, can be found from the normal distribution table, where:

$$Z=\frac{T-\dfrac{N(N+1)}{4}}{\sqrt{\dfrac{N(N+1)(2N+1)}{24}}}$$

Thus if N is 30, and T is calculated to be 100, then the Z score would be:

$$\frac{100-\dfrac{30\,.\,31}{4}}{\sqrt{\dfrac{30\,.\,31\,.\,61}{24}}}=\frac{100-232{\cdot}5}{\sqrt{2363{\cdot}75}}=-2{\cdot}725$$

Now table I shows the critical value of Z for 5 per cent significance to be 1·64 (one-tailed). As the observed value of Z exceeds this value the results would be judged significant at the 5 per cent level. (Note: Z will usually be negative using the above formula, but this does not affect its interpretation.)

The sign test

Choice of the test

The previous tests took account both of the direction of the difference between each pair of scores, and also of the *magnitude* of the difference. This is obviously reasonable when the scores represent a variable like 'volume of liquid consumed'. Thus it makes sense to say that the difference between the effects of the two drugs was greater for rat 9 (4 cc difference) than for rat 2 (1 cc difference). But what if the scores had represented ratings of 'beauty' or 'sincerity'? Suppose we had asked ten subjects each to rate the beauty of two paintings *A* and *B* on a scale from 0 to 10. We might find our results looking very much like those reported above for the drinking experiment. But it is doubtful whether the magnitude of the differences could now be taken so seriously. We would not wish to say that subject 9 (in place of rat 9) experienced a greater difference in the beauty of the two paintings than subject 2 (in place of rat 2). Obviously each subject might be using the scale in his own way, thereby invalidating any comparisons of the magnitude of differences. Nevertheless, the direction of each difference *is* meaningful. A subject who rates painting *A* as 5 and painting *B* as 7 presumably prefers *B*. So we *can* make use of the *directions* of the differences in order to assess whether painting *B* is judged significantly more beautiful than painting *A*. In these circumstances – provided, of course, we have a related samples design – we would make use of the sign test.

As with other non-parametric tests, the sign test may be used with data that would justify a more powerful test. Thus, we could use the sign test to analyse the experiment on drinking under the two drugs, but this would be wasteful of information and there would be a lower chance of reaching significance.

Rationale

The sign test simply makes use of the number of differences which are in one direction relative to the number which are in the other. If ten subjects each rate the two paintings *A* and *B*, we would expect about five subjects to prefer *A*, and about 5 to prefer *B* on a purely chance basis. If the 'split' was 6 for *A* and 4 for *B*, the null hypothesis of equal preference could hardly be rejected. But if as many as nine out of ten subjects, acting independently, gave higher ratings to *A* than *B*, then we might conclude that painting *A* produced *significantly* higher ratings than painting *B*. Using elementary probability theory (see, for example, Kolstoe, 1973, ch. 6) it is possible to calculate the chance of getting nine or more preferences for *A* under the null hypothesis that the subjects are drawn from a population in which *A* and *B* are equally popular. This is equivalent to calculating the probability of getting nine or more heads in ten tosses of a coin. If this probability is below 0·05 we may reject the null hypothesis that the two paintings are equally popular (or that the coin is fair) in favour of the alternate hypothesis that painting *A* induces significantly higher ratings than painting *B* (or that the coin is biased in favour of heads). The theoretical distribution underlying such situations is known as the *binomial distribution*. Tables of binomial probabilities may be used to determine the significance of the results.

Sign test: computation

GENERAL PROCEDURE

I Inspect the difference between each pair of scores. Put a plus sign (+) next to the differences in one direction, and a minus sign (−) next to the differences in the other direction.*

II Find the total number of either +s or −s, *whichever occurs less frequently*. Let this number be x.

III Find the critical value of x for the desired level of significance using table IV (p. 176). This value will depend upon (1) N, the total number of pairs, and (2) whether the prediction is directional.

IV If x is less than or equal to the critical value, reject the null hypothesis in favour of the alternate hypothesis that the independent variable has had an effect on behaviour.

* *Ties*. If a pair of scores are equal they should be dropped from the analysis, and the value of N reduced accordingly.

EXAMPLE

A comparison of ratings of beauty for two paintings. The experimenter predicts a difference between the ratings given to paintings *A* and *B*.

Subject	*Ratings of painting A* X_1	*Ratings of painting B* X_2	*Direction of difference* (X_1-X_2)
1	4	6	−
2	7	8	−
3	5	4	+
4	4	8	−
5	9	8	+
6	7	10	−
7	6	8	−
8	7	7	(omitted)
9	5	9	−
10	7	9	−

II Less frequent sign is +. x = number of +s = 2.

III Using table IV: The critical value of x for 5 per cent significance (two-tailed) is 1.

IV As the observed x value is larger than 1 we cannot reject the null hypothesis. There is no reason to assume that the paintings produce different responses in the subjects.

LARGE SAMPLES: *N* LARGER THAN 25

If N is larger than 25 table IV may not be used. However, the variable x, after certain corrections have been made, is normally distributed with a mean of $\frac{1}{2}N$ and a standard deviation of $\frac{1}{2}\sqrt{N}$. We can find the probability of obtaining a value as low or lower than x by using the normal distribution table, where

$$Z = \frac{\frac{1}{2}N - x - \frac{1}{2}}{\frac{1}{2}\sqrt{N}}$$

Thus if a sample of fifty subjects is tested in a repeated measures design, and if only ten subjects produce differences in one direction (and forty in the other), then the Z score is given by:

$$Z = \frac{\frac{1}{2}\times 50 - 10 - \frac{1}{2}}{\frac{1}{2}\sqrt{50}} = \frac{14{\cdot}5}{\frac{1}{2}\sqrt{50}} = 4{\cdot}101$$

Now table I shows the critical value of Z for significance at the 5 per cent level to be 1·64 (one-tailed). As the observed value of Z exceeds this value the results would be judged significant at the 5 per cent level.

Chapter summary

The tests described in this chapter apply to the analysis of differences between related samples of scores. The t-test and the Wilcoxon test are both powerful techniques since they take account of the direction of differences between the pairs of scores, and *also* the magnitude of these differences. The t-test makes additional assumptions about the normality of the data, which renders it slightly more powerful than the Wilcoxon when the normality assumptions are met. The sign test is a much cruder statistical technique, based only on the direction of the differences between pairs of scores. Nevertheless, this test may be the only possibility when the level of measurement is particularly crude. The relative power of the three tests is reflected in the outcomes to the three examples computed in the body of the chapter. Using identical data, 5 per cent significance was achieved with the t-test and the Wilcoxon, but with the sign test the p value was above 0·1.

6

One-sample tests

A one-sample experiment?

An experiment should involve the comparison of at least two sets of scores obtained under different experimental conditions. The idea is to vary the conditions (independent variable) and to examine the effects on the subjects' behaviour; so we may need to compare two, three or even more samples in the course of an experiment; but what, then, would be the purpose of testing just *one* sample of scores? The answer is a simple one. Suppose we already know how subjects perform in a given condition and we wish to examine the effects of changing that condition. It would be tedious – and sometimes impracticable – to reassess performance in the basic condition when an established norm already exists. So we would simply test a random sample of subjects in the modified condition and compare their performance with the previously established norm. We know, for example, that children have a mean score of 100 on certain standardized tests of reading ability. If a new method of teaching is introduced, we can assess its effectiveness by comparing the reading scores of a random sample of children taught by the new method with the previous norm of 100. Thus a one-sample test could be used to determine whether the performance of the sample was significantly better than the well-established norm of 100. A significant difference would imply an effect of teaching method even though only *one* condition has been directly investigated.

Difficulties of interpretation

The interpretation of a one-sample study is not, of course, quite as straightforward as that of a genuine experiment. The main problem is to know whether the single sample is equivalent, in terms of subject characteristics, to the original group on which the norm has been based. Unless the sample has been randomly selected from that group – call it the population – there will be difficulty in pinning down the cause of any difference that is obtained. For example, a significant improvement in the reading scores might be due to the new method of teaching, but it could also occur if the sample contained brighter children than the population on which the norm was based. Even if the sample matched the population perfectly with regard to background characteristics, it might well have been influenced by the 'Hawthorne Effect' – that is, the tendency for individuals to respond to special attention or a change in routine. Thus the subjects taught to read by the new method might become more highly motivated simply because they felt themselves to be involved in something new, irrespective of the nature of the teaching method itself. These kinds of effect make it very difficult to achieve experimental rigour in a one-sample design unless the sample and population are properly matched in all respects – a condition which is virtually unattainable.

Non-experimental use of one-sample tests

Problems of matching do not arise when the intention is to compare the performance of one *type* of subject in the sample with that of another type of subject in the population. For example, we might wish to know whether airline pilots have faster reaction times than the general population of adult males, or whether extroverts change their jobs more frequently than others. Such questions can be answered by comparing the relevant sample mean with a previously established mean for the population. There is no pretence here to show a *causal* connection between the type of subject and the response measure, but only a *correlation* which could be mediated in many different ways. Thus although extroverts may change their jobs more frequently than others, we cannot say whether this is because they are extroverts or because of some other factor related to extroversion. By accepting this more modest conclusion we do not have to assume that sample and population are perfectly matched on all but one variable as we did in the experimental study of teaching methods.

Testing a sample against a theoretical population

Perhaps the most straightforward case of all occurs when we wish to compare the performance of a sample with a mean score based on a theory of some kind rather than on past measurement. Suppose, for example, we wished to teach children to discriminate between nouns and verbs. Before training we would expect such children to achieve half-marks in a test that required them to classify a set of words into nouns and verbs, i.e. they should get half right by chance if they had no idea how to perform the task and had to guess. In order to discover whether the teaching was successful we should therefore compare the actual scores of our sample after training, with the mean score of an untrained population – that is, 50 per cent. In this case there is also no problem of interpretation – if the sample mean is significantly greater than the level of performance expected by chance, then the training has been effective.

The relation between the sample and the population

From what has been said so far it should be clear that the sample does not have to be a physical part of the population in order for a statistical comparison to be made. All of the following examples qualify for a one-sample test, although only in the first case is the sample actually part of the population.

(1) Is the mean IQ of a random sample of psychologists higher than the mean IQ of university graduates generally?

(2) Is the mean income of a random sample of female doctors lower than the previously established mean income for all male doctors?
(3) Is the mean score of a sample of 'psychics' on an ESP test higher than the mean of the population of scores that would be expected by chance?

What is being tested in each of these cases is whether the *statistical* properties of the sample are significantly different from the *statistical* properties of the population. The physical relationship between the sample and population is irrelevant in this context.

We shall now consider three tests that may be used to compare sample and population parameters:

the one-sample Z test (parametric)
the one-sample t-test (parametric)
the one-sample proportions test (non-parametric)

The one-sample Z test

Choice of test

This is the one-sample analog of the two-sample Z test and is used to determine whether a sample mean is significantly different from the mean of some specified population of scores. The usual parametric assumptions are made, namely that the scores in the sample come from a normal population and meet the requirements of an interval scale of measurement. In addition the Z formula takes account of the *standard deviation* of the population with which the sample is being compared. If this standard deviation is not known it may be replaced by the standard deviation of the sample scores themselves, but only if the sample is large ($\geqslant 30$).

To summarize, the Z test may be used if:

(1) sample scores come from a normal (or near normal) population;
(2) measurement is on an interval scale; and
(3) population standard deviation is known *or* sample size is at least thirty.

Rationale

In essence, the Z test measures the probability that the sample could have been obtained by random selection from a given population of scores. The Z value represents, in standardized form, the size of the difference between the sample mean and the population mean. Hence the *larger* the Z value, the *lower* is the probability that the sample came from the specified population. If the probability falls below the critical value required for significance (say 0·05) then the sample is presumed to come from a different population with a different mean. The derivation of the Z formula was described earlier (see p. 71–3).

One-sample Z test: computation

GENERAL PROCEDURE

I Let μ be the mean of the population.
Calculate the mean of the sample, $\bar{X}$, using

$$\bar{X}=\frac{\Sigma X}{N}$$

where N is the sample size.

II Let σ be the standard deviation of the population.
If σ is not known, then calculate the standard deviation of the sample of scores (s), using the formula:

$$S=\sqrt{\frac{\Sigma X^2}{N}-\bar{X}^2}$$

$$\left(\text{or } S=\sqrt{\frac{\Sigma fX^2}{N}-\bar{X}^2}, \text{ for grouped data}\right)$$

III Substitute the values of X, μ, N and σ (or S) into the formula:

$$Z=\frac{\bar{X}-\mu}{\frac{\sigma}{\sqrt{N}}} \quad \left(\text{or, if } \sigma \text{ is not known, use } Z=\frac{\bar{X}-\mu}{\frac{S}{\sqrt{N}}}\right)$$

IV Convert Z into a probability that the sample has been randomly selected from the population. Use the normal distribution tables, p. 172–3. (If the test is two-tailed the probability shown in the tables should be doubled.)

V If the probability falls below the critical value for significance (say 0·05) we may reject the null hypothesis that the sample comes from the specified population. Instead, we conclude that the sample comes from a different population with regard to its mean.

EXAMPLE

Performance on a selection test is known to be normally distributed with a mean score for all applicants of 28 and with a standard deviation of 5 points. An investigator wishes to determine whether late applicants have significantly lower scores on the test than the general population of applicants.

Test scores of a random sample of late applicants ($N=25$)
24, 27, 29, 30, 32, 26, 25, 26, 29, 30
28, 29, 26, 28, 27, 28, 30, 33, 22, 24
31, 20, 18, 35, 26

I Population mean, $\mu=28$ (given)

$$\text{Sample mean, } \bar{X}=\frac{\Sigma X}{N}=\frac{24+27+\ldots+35+26}{25}$$

$$=\frac{683}{25}=27{\cdot}32$$

II Population standard deviation, $\sigma=5$ (given).
(If σ had not been specified, the sample standard deviation, S, would be calculated and used in its place.)

$$\text{III } Z=\frac{27{\cdot}32-28{\cdot}00}{\frac{5}{\sqrt{25}}}=\frac{-0{\cdot}68}{\frac{5}{5}}=-0{\cdot}68$$

IV We can ignore the minus sign. It shows that the sample mean is *smaller* than the population mean, but has no bearing on the magnitude of the difference.

Using table I: A Z value of 0·68 corresponds to a probability of 0·248. (As the test is one-tailed this probability is not adjusted.)

V *Conclusion.* A random sample from the general population of applicants' scores is quite likely to have a mean as low as – or lower than – 27·32. The probability of getting such a sample from the population is almost 25 per cent. Hence the results are *not* significant and we cannot conclude that late applicants have lower scores than the general population of applicants.

The one-sample t-test

Choice of test

The one-sample t-test is used to compare the mean of a sample of scores with the mean of a specified population from which the sample may have been drawn. For example, the t-test could be used to compare the mean score of a random sample of professors on a memory test with a previously obtained mean for a large population of normal adults. The purpose is to discover whether the sample can be regarded as being randomly selected from the specified population, or whether it is likely to have come from another population with a different mean.

Like the Z test, the t-test is parametric; it assumes an interval level of measurement and also that the sample has been drawn from a normal population, but this requirement can be relaxed. Unlike the Z test, the t-test does not require a large sample, nor does it assume that the standard deviation of the population is known. Thus the t-test can be used when the Z test cannot, i.e. with a small sample and an unknown population standard deviation.

Rationale

The t-test measures the probability that a sample of scores could have been obtained by random selection from a given population. The value of t increases as the difference between the sample and population means increases. Thus a large t value implies a large difference between the sample and population and therefore a *low* probability that the sample comes from the population. If the probability falls below the critical value required for significance (say 0·05) then the sample is presumed to come from a different population with a different mean. The derivation of the t formula is described in some detail in chapter 4 (see pp. 83–4).

The translation of the t value into a probability depends on the degrees of freedom (see p. 174) in the test. For a one-sample test the degrees of freedom are *one less* than the sample size.

One sample t-test: computation

GENERAL PROCEDURE

I Let μ be the mean of the population.
Calculate the mean of the sample, $\bar{X}$, using

$$\bar{X} = \frac{\Sigma X}{N}$$

where N is the sample size.

II Calculate the standard deviation of the sample, S, using the formula:

$$S = \sqrt{\frac{\Sigma X^2}{N} - \bar{X}^2}$$

III Substitute the values of $\bar{X}$, μ, N and S into the t formula:

$$t_{N-1} = \frac{\bar{X} - \mu}{\dfrac{S}{\sqrt{N-1}}}$$

IV Find the number of degrees of freedom from the formula: $df = N - 1$

V Find the value of t needed to achieve your selected level of significance using table II, p. 174. The critical value will depend on (1) the degrees of freedom, and (2) whether the prediction is one- or two-tailed.

VI If the observed value of t is *equal* to, or *greater* than, the critical value, we may reject the null hypothesis and conclude that the sample does *not* come from the population specified in the test.

EXAMPLE

The mean time required to answer a questionnaire is known to be 13·5 minutes and the distribution is normal. A modified version is developed and the designer wishes to test whether the completion time has changed significantly.

Time required to complete the modified questionnaire by a random sample of 20 *respondents* (time in minutes)
17, 18, 21, 12, 16, 9, 13, 17, 14, 15
11, 14, 7, 18, 19, 9, 17, 19, 20, 18

I Population mean, $\mu = 13{\cdot}5$ minutes (given).

$$\text{Sample mean, } \bar{X} = \frac{\Sigma X}{N} = \frac{17+18+\ldots+20+18}{20}$$

$$= \frac{304}{20} = 15{\cdot}2 \text{ minutes}$$

II Sample standard deviation,

$$S = \sqrt{\frac{\Sigma X^2}{N} - \bar{X}^2}$$

$$= \sqrt{\frac{17^2+18^2+\ldots+20^2+18^2}{20} - 15{\cdot}2^2}$$

$$= \sqrt{\frac{4920}{20} - 15{\cdot}2^2} = 3{\cdot}868$$

III $$t_{N-1} = \frac{\bar{X}-\mu}{\dfrac{S}{\sqrt{N-1}}} = \frac{15{\cdot}2-13{\cdot}5}{\dfrac{3{\cdot}868}{\sqrt{19}}} = 1{\cdot}916$$

IV $df = 20-1 = 19$

V Using table II: For 19 degrees of freedom the value of t required for the 5 per cent level of significance (two-tailed) is 2·093.

VI *Conclusion.* The observed value of t is just less than 2·093 and the results are therefore not quite significant at the 5 per cent level. We do not have enough evidence to conclude that the modified questionnaire requires a significantly different completion time (i.e. this sample of completion times could have come from the original population with a mean of 13·5 minutes).

The one-sample proportions test

Choice of test

The mean is not the only attribute of a sample that may be of interest. If the behaviour we are studying is on a nominal scale (e.g. happy/sad, agree/disagree, etc.) we cannot represent the average score of the group by a mean, but only by a proportion. Thus a sample in which the proportion of happy people is 0·8 could be regarded as happier than a sample in which only 0·5 of the members are happy.

Now just as we might want to compare a sample mean with a population mean, so we might want to compare a sample proportion with a population proportion. Here are some example comparisons which make the point more clearly:

Is the proportion of vegetarians in a random sample of clergymen higher than the proportion of vegetarians in the general population?

Is the proportion of men in a random sample of smokers greater than 0·5? (This being the proportion expected under the hypothesis that men and women have an equal propensity to smoke.)

A random sample of patients is treated with a new drug. Is the proportion of patients in this sample who recover within a month higher than the proportion that used to recover under the old drug?

In each of these cases a one-sample test will determine whether the proportion in the sample differs significantly from a specified population proportion. As with tests on means, the population proportion may be based on a theory of some kind, or it may have been established by empirical research. In both cases the intention is to see whether the sample could feasibly be regarded as a random sample from the population. The only assumptions of the test are that the measurements constitute a dichotomy (e.g. smokes/doesn't smoke) and that at least ten subjects would be *expected* to fall into each category if the population proportion was true of the sample. Suppose, for example, that the proportion of smokers in a population was 0·8 and that a random sample of fifty was to be compared with the population. If the population proportion is applied to the sample we expect to find 40 smokers (0·8 × 50) and 10 non-smokers (0·2 × 50) in the sample. Since both of these frequencies are at least 10 we may proceed with the test. However, if the population proportion was 0·9, a sample of size 50 would be too small to qualify for the test because the expected number of non-smokers would be only 5 (0·1 × 50). Note that the actual number of smokers and non-smokers in the sample is irrelevant, it is only the *expected* numbers, based on the population proportion, that count.

Rationale

The one-sample proportion test is technically non-parametric because it does not assume normality or interval scaling. Nevertheless, the test statistic turns out to be a Z score with a similar interpretation to the Z obtained in the one-sample Z test. Thus the magnitude of the difference between the sample proportion and the population proportion is represented by Z. A large value of Z corresponds to a low probability that the sample could have been randomly selected from the population. If this probability is below 0·05 (or another chosen level) we conclude that the observed proportion in the sample could not have arisen by random sampling of the population. The sample is then presumed to come from another population with a different characteristic proportion.

One-sample test: computation

GENERAL PROCEDURE

I Let P be the proportion in the population with a given characteristic.
Let p be the proportion in the sample with this characteristic.
Let N be the sample size.

II To check whether the test can be applied:
Calculate the *expected* number in the sample with the characteristic.
This is $N \times P$.
Calculate the *expected* number without the characteristic.
This is $N(1-P)$.
If $N \times P \geqslant 10$ and $N(1-P) \geqslant 10$, then the test may be applied.
(Note: this is just an algebraic statement of the rules given under *Choice of test*.)

III Substitute the values of P, p and N into the formula:

$$Z = \frac{p-P}{\sqrt{\dfrac{P(1-P)}{N}}}$$

IV Convert Z into a probability that the sample has been randomly selected from the population. Use the normal distribution tables, pp. 172–3. (If the test is two-tailed the probability shown in the tables should be doubled.)

V If the probability falls below the critical value for significance (say 0·05), we may reject the null hypothesis that the sample comes from the specified population. Instead, we conclude that the sample comes from a population with a different proportion of individuals having the characteristic.

EXAMPLE

The proportion of science students who are female is 0·3. After a publicity campaign designed to attract women into science a random sample of ninety science students is found to contain forty females. Does this constitute a significant rise in the proportion of female science students?

I $P=0{\cdot}3,\ p=\frac{40}{90}=0{\cdot}444,\ N=90$

II Expected number of female scientists (using population proportion) is given by: $N \times P = 90 \times 0{\cdot}3 = 27$
Expected number of male scientists $= N(1-P) = 90 \times 0{\cdot}7 = 63$
Both expected frequencies exceed 10, therefore test can be performed.

III $$Z = \frac{p-P}{\sqrt{\frac{P(1-P)}{N}}} = \frac{0{\cdot}444 - 0{\cdot}3}{\sqrt{\frac{0{\cdot}3 \times 0{\cdot}7}{90}}} = \frac{0{\cdot}1444}{0{\cdot}0483} = 2{\cdot}99$$

IV Using table I: A Z value of 2·99 corresponds to a probability of 0·0014. (As the test is one-tailed this probability is not adjusted.)

V *Conclusion.* The probability of obtaining a sample proportion as high as 0·444 from a population with proportion 0·3 is very low. Hence it is very unlikely that this sample could have been drawn randomly from the population of science students that existed before the publicity campaign. Instead we conclude that the true proportion of science students who are female is significantly greater than 0·3 after the campaign.
(Note: we have *not* demonstrated a causal connection between the campaign and the increased proportion of female scientists. The difference may have been caused by some other factor linked to the campaign, e.g. the passage of time.)

Chapter summary

The tests described in this chapter examine whether an observed sample of scores could have come from a specified population. The features of the population are either defined *a priori*, for example on the basis of a theory, or they are established from previous research on very large numbers of subjects. The one-sample Z test assesses the probability that the sample has been randomly selected from a population with a specified mean. It assumes (1) interval data, (2) normality and (3) *either* a large sample *or* knowledge of the population standard deviation.

The t-test has the same function as the Z test and makes the same assumptions except that (3) is omitted. Both tests are parametric, but the Z test is naturally more powerful than t.

The one-sample proportions test assesses whether a sample could have been randomly selected from a population with a specified proportion of elements having some characteristic. It is non-parametric and assumes only that the measures are nominal and that the sample size meets certain criteria (see p. 121).

7

Tests for trend and spread

Trend tests for three or more samples

The main emphasis in this book has been on the analysis of two-sample designs. It is however desirable to extend these designs in order to be able to compare the effects of three or more levels of the independent variable. The circumstances under which this might be done are discussed in the final chapter.

Once we have more than two conditions in the experiment the range of possible predictions is increased. Suppose we conduct an experiment to compare rate of learning of three tasks, A, B and C. One prediction might be that we expect a difference between at least two of these conditions. This is the most general prediction we could make. Alternatively we could predict a *trend* such that performance in task C is better than performance in task B, which in turn is better than performance in task A. The designs which might be used in such experiments are analogous to those described in chapter 1 in the two-sample case. Thus we could have the same group of subjects performing under all three (or k) treatments – a related k-sample design; or we could compare the performance of separate, randomly selected groups of subjects – an independent k-sample design. The choice between these alternatives depends on precisely the same considerations that were discussed in connection with two-sample designs.

The statistical analysis of k-sample designs is generally far beyond the scope of this book, involving more complex procedures such as *analysis of variance*, which are discussed in more advanced texts. (For a good introduction to analysis of variance, see Meddis, 1973). However since the use of k-sample designs is extremely common in introductory experimental work a brief summary of the computational procedures for k-sample *trend* tests has been included here. Further details and derivations are given in Page (1963) and Jonckheere (1954).

Jonckheere trend test for independent samples

This is a non-parametric test assuming an ordinal level of measurement. The test may be used to evaluate a predicted trend across the k groups of scores, where k has a maximum value of 6. This presentation assumes equal numbers of subjects in each sample, but the test may be generalized to designs with unequal sample sizes.

GENERAL PROCEDURE

I Arrange the samples of scores in the *predicted* order, from the lowest scores on the left, to the highest scores on the right.

II Write next to each score the number of scores *in all the columns to the right* that *exceed* the value of the score being considered. (Note: the final column will not have any scores to the right.) When counting the number of scores which exceed each score do *not* include ties.

III Find the sum of the figures obtained in II. Let this sum be A.

IV Now find the maximum value that A could take (B) using the formula:

$$B = \frac{k(k-1)}{2} N^2$$

where N = number of scores *in each sample*,
k = number *of* samples.

V Substitute A and B in the following formula and compute S the test statistic:

$S = 2A - B$

(Note: if there is no trend the expected value of S is zero; the more marked the trend, the larger the value of S.)

VI Find the critical value of S for the desired level of significance using table IX, p. 180. The tabled values assume that the direction of trend was predicted. The critical value will depend on k and N.

VII If the observed value of S is larger than, or equal to, the critical value reject the null hypothesis in favour of the alternate hypothesis that there is a trend across the k samples of scores.

EXAMPLE

The relationship between degree of neuroticism and errors in a learning task. The experimenter predicts an increase in the error rates from low to middle to high levels of neuroticism ($N = 5$ for each group).

Low		*Medium*		*High*
2	(10)	5	(5)	11
3	(10)	4	(5)	6
1	(10)	6	(4)	8
4	(8)	4	(5)	9
2	(10)	9	(1)	7
	↑		↑	

Number of times scores are exceeded by values to the right

III $A = 10 + 10 + 10 + 8 + 10 + 5 + 5 + 4 + 5 + 1$
$= 68$

IV $B = \frac{k(k-1)}{2} N^2 = \frac{3 \times 2}{2} \times 5^2 = 75$

V $S = 2A - B = 2 \times 68 - 75 = 61$

VI Using table IX: For $k = 3$, $N = 5$, the minimum value of S required for significance at the 5 per cent level is 33.

VII *Conclusion*. As the observed value of S exceeds 33, we can conclude that there is a significant trend across the three groups of scores.

Page's L *trend test for related samples*

This is a non-parametric test assuming an ordinal level of measurement. The test may be used to evaluate a predicted trend across k-related samples.

GENERAL PROCEDURE

I Arrange the samples of scores in the *predicted* order from the lowest scores on the left, to the highest on the right.

II Let k = number of related samples; and let N = number of subjects.

III Rank the scores in each *row* of the table (i.e. for each subject) in order from lowest score (=1) to highest score (= k).

IV Add together the rankings in each *column*. Call these totals R values.

V Find ΣRu, where u is the number of each column from 1 (on extreme left) to k (on extreme right). Let $L = \Sigma Ru$.

VI Find the critical value of L for the desired significance level using table X, p. 181. The tabled values assume the direction of trend was predicted. The critical value will depend on k and N.

VII If the observed value of L is larger than, or equal to, the critical value, reject the null hypothesis in favour of the alternate hypothesis that there is a trend across the k samples of scores.

EXAMPLE

The relationship between level of reward and 'hits' in an aiming task. The experimenter predicts that hit rate will increase with level of reward (N=4).

u	1	2	3
	Low	*Medium*	*High*
Figures in	4 (1)	7 (2)	11 (3)
brackets are	6 (2)	4 (1)	8 (3)
rankings	3 (1)	5 (2)	6 (3)
	2 (1)	7 (2)	9 (3)
IV R	5	7	12

V $\Sigma Ru = (5 \times 1) + (7 \times 2) + (12 \times 3) = 5 + 14 + 36 = 55 = L$

VI Using table X: For $k=3$, $N=4$, the minimum value of L required for significance at the 5 per cent level is 54.

VII *Conclusion.* As the observed value of L exceeds 54, we can conclude that there is a significant trend across the three groups of scores.

Testing for differences between variances

The vast majority of psychological theories lead to predictions about the effect of independent variables on the *level* of a subject's performance. In order to compare the levels of performance under various conditions we normally conduct tests on differences between means or other measures of central tendency. It sometimes happens, however, that we can make a prediction about changes in the *variability* of performance under the different conditions of an experiment. For example, rather than predict a drop in the level of mental performance during noise (a prediction about means), we might expect the subjects to become more *variable* in their performance under noisy conditions. In this case we could conduct an identical experiment to that devised in chapter 2. We would again measure the performance of two independent groups under different levels of noise, but this time we would wish to test for a difference between some measure of the variability of the groups, rather than their means. If we can assume that the two samples are drawn from normal populations of scores, we can test the hypothesis about differences in variability using an F-test.

We might also use this test as a preliminary to the computation of a t-test. In this case we would be using it to discover whether the assumption of homogeneity of variance (equal variance) was violated by our data. If it was not, we would be justified in continuing with the t-test.

Neither of the above applications would justify the inclusion of the F-test in this short, introductory text. However, the test has a much more important function in the branch of statistics known as *analysis of variance.* Since analysis of variance techniques are particularly useful in experimental psychology, and will be met at more advanced levels, the basic idea of the F-test will be introduced here.

Rationale

Suppose we wish to decide whether two samples with differing variances could have been drawn by chance from a single population (or two populations with the same variance). We could adopt the same strategy that was used in developing the t-test (see p. 71). We begin by considering the repeated sampling of a hypothetical population, draw up the sampling distribution for the property we are interested in, and then use this to decide whether any observed value, or difference in values, could be obtained by chance from the specified population. If this procedure is followed in the case of differences between sample variances, it can be shown that the *ratio* of the two sample variances follows a distribution known as F. This distribution can then be used to determine the probability of obtaining a difference as large or larger than the observed difference by chance. The test assumes normality of the underlying population distribution and interval measurement.

F-test: computation

GENERAL PROCEDURE

I Let S_1^2 and S_2^2 be the two variances; let N_1 and N_2 be the corresponding sample sizes.

II Calculate the values of S_1^2 and S_2^2 using the formula:

$$S^2 = \frac{\Sigma X^2}{N} - \bar{X}^2$$

III Find: $A = S_1^2 \times \frac{N_1}{N_1 - 1}$ $\quad B = S_2^2 \times \frac{N_2}{N_2 - 1}$

Then calculate: $F = A/B$ or B/A, whichever is the larger.

IV Find the critical value of F for the desired level of significance using table VIII, pp. 178–9. This value will depend on: (1) the degrees of freedom for the numerator [$(N_1 - 1)$ if the numerator is A] and the degrees of freedom for the denominator [$(N_2 - 1)$ if the denominator is B] of the F ratio; and (2) whether the experimenter predicted which sample would have the larger variance in advance.

V If the value of F is larger than or equal to the critical value, reject the null hypothesis in favour of the alternate hypothesis that the independent variable has produced a difference in the variance of the two groups of scores.

EXAMPLE

Effect of noise on the variability of performance in a cognitive task. The experimenter predicts that performance will be more variable under noise ($N_1 = 10$, $N_2 = 8$).

I

Scores under noise conditions		*Scores under no noise conditions*	
X_1	X_1^2	X_2	X_2^2
8	64	4	16
4	14	5	25
6	36	6	36
7	49	5	25
5	25	6	36
6	36	4	16
9	81	7	49
10	100	5	25
8	64		
4	16		
$\Sigma X_1 = 67$	$\Sigma X_1^2 = 485$	$\Sigma X_2 = 42$	$\Sigma X_2^2 = 228$

II $\bar{X}_1 = \frac{\Sigma X_1}{N_1} = \frac{67}{10} = 6{\cdot}7$ $\qquad \bar{X}_2 = \frac{\Sigma X_2}{N_2} = \frac{42}{8} = 5{\cdot}25$

$$S_1^2 = \frac{\Sigma X_1^2}{N_1} - \bar{X}_1^2 = \frac{485}{10} - 6{\cdot}7^2 = 3{\cdot}61$$

$$S_2^2 = \frac{\Sigma X_2^2}{N_2} - \bar{X}_2^2 = \frac{228}{8} - 5{\cdot}25^2 = 0{\cdot}9375$$

III $A = S_1^2 \times \frac{N_1}{N_1 - 1} = 3{\cdot}61 \times \frac{10}{9} = 4{\cdot}011$

$$B = S_2^2 \times \frac{N_2}{N_2 - 1} = 0{\cdot}9375 \times \frac{8}{7} = 1{\cdot}071$$

$$F = \frac{A}{B} = \frac{4{\cdot}011}{1{\cdot}071} = 3{\cdot}75$$

IV Using table VIII: For $(N_1-1)=9$, $(N_2-1)=7$ the critical value of F for significance at the 5 per cent level (one-tailed) is 3·68.

V As the observed value of F exceeds 3·68, we can conclude that there is a significant difference between the variances of the two samples.
(Note: if the tables do not give the critical value of F for the degrees of freedom you require, use the next *lowest* values of *df* given in the table. For example, if the degrees of freedom were 14, 32 you would look up the critical value of F for $df=12, 30$. This procedure reduces the level of significance very slightly, i.e. the test becomes more *conservative*. But this is preferable to rounding up the values of the *df* which would artificially boost the significance of the results.)

8 Measuring the relationship between two variables

Correlation

In Chapter 1 a distinction was drawn between experimental and correlational research: in an experiment we *manipulate* one variable and *measure* the consequential changes in another variable; in a correlational study we *measure* both variables – that is, we try to relate naturally occurring variations in one variable, say income, to naturally occurring variations in another, say intelligence. Thus experiments lead to the discovery of direct, *causal* connections between variables whereas correlations may be mediated by a string of intervening variables and do not necessarily reflect causation at all. None the less, correlational research can yield interesting and theoretically useful findings in circumstances where experimental manipulations would be impossible, e.g. where social and personality variables are being studied (see p. 6).

To obtain the correlation between such variables, say, income and intelligence, we would measure the IQs and incomes of a large sample of people, and then inspect the data to see if people with high IQs also tended to have the high incomes, and people with low IQs, low incomes. A good way to present the results of such a study is by means of a *scattergram* – that is, a graph in which the two scores of each person are represented by a dot. The coordinates of each dot on the horizontal (X) axis and the vertical (Y) axis would represent that person's scores on the two variables, IQ and income. By looking at the complete pattern of dots we get a visual impression of the degree to which the two variables are correlated with each other. Some possible outcomes are shown in figure 16. In figure 16(a) there is a *high, positive* correlation – the dots are closely packed around an imaginary line representing an increase in intelligence with income. In figure 16(b) the correlation is equally high, but this time *negative* – as one variable increases, the other decreases.

Figures 16(c) and (d) show weaker positive and negative correlations – the dots are less closely packed around the line relating IQ to income. Another way of saying this is that it would be more difficult to *predict* a person's score on one variable from a knowledge of his score on the other in the situations represented in figures 16(c) and (d). Finally, figures 16(e) and (f) represent the complete absence of a linear correlation between two variables. In figure 16(e) there is no relationship at all, but in (f) there is a very strong *non-linear* relationship between the variables. In the latter situation the usual measures of correlation do not apply, since these only detect linear relationships.

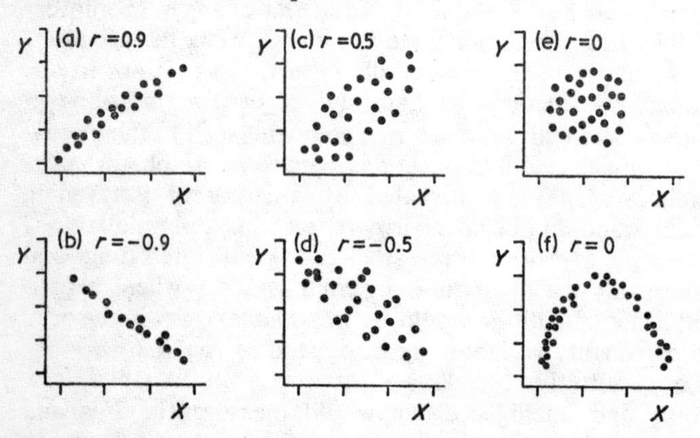

Figure 16 Scattergrams illustrating different types of relationship between two variables

Measures of correlation

Although inspection of a scattergram gives a clear impression of the degree of relationship between two variables, we often want to quantify this more precisely using a single numerical index that will allow us to compare the strength of several different correlations. To do this we calculate the descriptive statistic known as the *coefficient of correlation*, usually represented by r. There are a number of different procedures for calculating r, but they all yield a measure which varies on a scale between $+1$ and -1. The size of the coefficient represents the *degree* of relationship, and the sign represents the *direction* of the relationship. Thus an r of $+1$ is obtained for a perfect, positive correlation, -1 signifies a perfect, negative correlation, and an r of zero is obtained when there is no linear relationship between the two variables. Appropriate values of r for the data in figure 16 are shown at the top of each scattergram. As shown in figure 16(f) an r of zero does not necessarily imply *no* relationship between the variables, only that there is no linear relationship.

The product–moment correlation coefficient (Pearson *r*)

The Pearson r is the most commonly used measure of correlation. It represents the strength of the *linear* relationship between two variables and can only be properly applied in cases where both variables are measured on an interval or ratio scale (p. 62). Thus one could use the product–moment correlation coefficient to assess the strength of the relationship between the height and the weight of a set of individuals, but not the relationship beween their level of extroversion and their self-confidence.

As indicated above, the r value varies between $+1$ and -1. A positive value means that individuals obtaining high scores on one variable will tend to have high scores on the other. Similarly, those subjects having low scores on one variable will tend to have low scores on the other. A negative r value indicates the reverse pattern: high scores on one variable go with low scores on the other.

We shall not discuss the statistical basis of the correlation coefficient, but there are two general ideas about the meaning of r which are worth noting:

(1) r may be thought of as measuring the amount of spread of the points in a scattergram around an imaginary line going through the centre of these points. Reference to figure 16 will illustrate the idea that the closer the points are to the imaginary line, the larger the value of r. When r is $+1$ (or -1) the points all fall exactly on a line. In this case a person's score on Y can be predicted perfectly from his or her score on X.

(2) If the value of r is squared the resulting statistic is known as the *coefficient of determination*. This indicates the proportion of the variation in the Y scores that can be accounted for by knowing X. For example, if the correlation between a child's height and age is 0·8 then 64 per cent ($0{\cdot}8^2 \times 100$) of the variation in children's heights can be predicted by knowing their ages. Obviously a perfect correlation allows one to predict all the variation in Y from a knowledge of the subjects' X scores since when $r=1$, $r^2 \times 100 = 100$ per cent.

Pearson r: computation

GENERAL PROCEDURE

I Draw a scattergram. This will give you a good idea whether the relationship is linear. (If it is obviously non-linear stop here.) The scattergram also tells you whether to expect a positive or negative correlation and whether to expect a high or a low value.

II Set out the two measures for each of the subjects as follows:

	X	Y	XY	X^2	Y^2
S_1	—	—			
S_2	—	—			
S_3	—	—			
·	·	·			
·	·	·			
·	·	·			
S_N	—	—			
	ΣX	ΣY	ΣXY	ΣX^2	ΣY^2

Call the independent or causative variable X, and the dependent variable Y (e.g. in a correlation between children's ages and heights, X would represent age and Y

would represent height since age determines height).*

III Fill in the rest of the table shown in II. The XY column contains the products of each subject's X and Y scores. The X^2 and Y^2 columns contain the squares of each subject's two scores.

IV Find the totals of the entries in each column, i.e. ΣX, ΣY, ΣXY, ΣX^2, ΣY^2.

V Substitute these totals together with the value for N (the number of subjects) into the formula for r:

$$r = \frac{\Sigma XY - \dfrac{(\Sigma X)(\Sigma Y)}{N}}{\sqrt{\left(\Sigma X^2 - \dfrac{(\Sigma X)^2}{N}\right)\left(\Sigma Y^2 - \dfrac{(\Sigma Y)^2}{N}\right)}}$$

VI r is then an index of the strength of the linear relationship between X and Y. To check whether the observed relationship is a reliable one (i.e. significantly above zero) use table XI. The critical value, p. 182, of r required for significance will depend on (1) N and (2) whether the test is one- or two-tailed, i.e. whether the direction of the correlation – positive or negative – was predicted.

EXAMPLE

The relationship between children's ages and their reading speeds (words read in 30 seconds). The experimenter predicts a positive correlation for children in the 5–12 years age range.

	S_1	S_2	S_3	S_4	S_5	S_6	S_7	S_8	S_9	S_{10}
Age (years)	5	7	6	8	9	5	10	6	8	9
Words read in 30 secs	7	9	8	11	11	6	13	8	9	12

I Scattergram

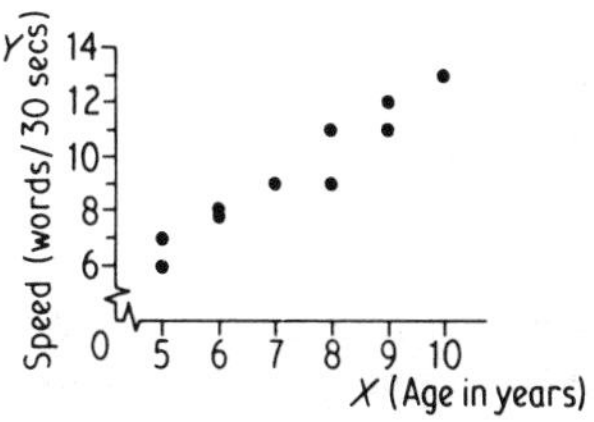

* If neither variable can be regarded as the cause or predictor of the other then either variable may be treated as X and the other as Y.

The scattergram leads us to expect a strong, positive correlation. The relationship is clearly linear and suitable for Pearson *r*.

II and III

	X	Y	XY	X^2	Y^2
S_1	5	7	35	25	49
S_2	7	9	63	49	81
S_3	6	8	48	36	64
S_4	8	11	88	64	121
S_5	9	11	99	81	121
S_6	5	6	30	25	36
S_7	10	13	130	100	169
S_8	6	8	48	36	64
S_9	8	9	72	64	81
S_{10}	9	12	108	81	144
IV	$\Sigma X=73$	$\Sigma Y=94$	$\Sigma XY=72$	$\Sigma X^2=561$	$\Sigma Y^2=930$

V
$$r=\frac{\Sigma XY-\frac{(\Sigma X)(\Sigma Y)}{N}}{\sqrt{\left(\Sigma X^2-\frac{(\Sigma X)^2}{N}\right)\left(\Sigma Y^2-\frac{(\Sigma Y)^2}{N}\right)}}$$

$$=\frac{721-\frac{73\times 94}{10}}{\sqrt{\left(561-\frac{73^2}{10}\right)\left(930-\frac{94^2}{10}\right)}}$$

$$=\frac{721-686{\cdot}2}{\sqrt{(561-532{\cdot}9)(930-883{\cdot}6)}}$$

$$=\frac{34{\cdot}80}{\sqrt{28{\cdot}1\times 46{\cdot}4}}=\frac{34{\cdot}80}{36{\cdot}11}=0{\cdot}964$$

VI Using table XI: The critical value of *r* for 1 per cent significance (one-tailed) is 0·716. As the observed *r* exceeds this value, we conclude that there is a highly significant positive correlation between age and reading speed in children.

Spearman's rank order correlation (r_s)

In our previous discussion we emphasized the use of r as an index of a linear relationship between two variables. But in most psychological research, particularly where a correlation is being used in preference to an experiment, the variables are not measureable on an interval scale, i.e. in standard units. Variables like extraversion, neuroticism or creativity are, at best, measured on an ordinal scale. The idea of a *linear* relationship between two such variables does not really make sense because of the lack of uniform scaling. However it does make sense to consider a more general question, namely whether one variable tends to increase (or decrease) as the other increases – that is, whether the relationship is *monotonic*. A linear relationship is a special case of the more general, monotonic relationship between two variables.

Spearman's r_s is a non-parametric coefficient of correlation which is specifically designed to measure the degree of a monotonic relationship between two variables. It is used with data which are in the form of ranks, or can be meaningfully converted to ranks.

The scattergrams below show various relationships which are all non-linear. However some of them are perfect monotonic relationships, i.e. those in which an increase in X is always associated with an increase (or in some cases decrease) in Y. Scattergrams (a) and (b) both illustrate perfect positive monotonic relationships and the data would produce an r_s value of 1. Scattergram (c) shows a perfect negative monotonic trend and would be described by $r_s = -1$. Scattergram (d)

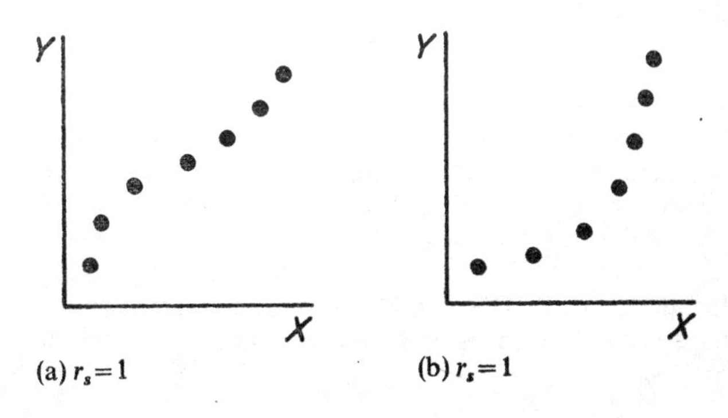

(a) $r_s = 1$ (b) $r_s = 1$

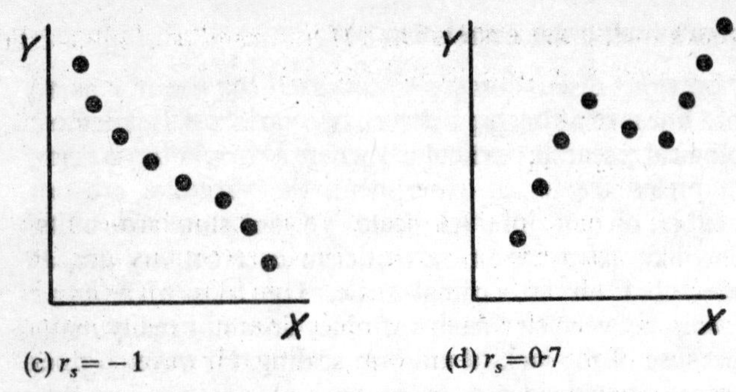

(c) $r_s = -1$ (d) $r_s = 0{\cdot}7$

illustrates a reverse in the upward trend leading to an imperfect monotonic relationship. The expected r_s value would therefore be *less than* 1.

Rationale

If two variables are correlated we would expect those people who obtain the lower scores on one variable to obtain the lower scores on the other, and those who have high scores on one variable to obtain high scores on the other. In calculating Spearman's *r*, all we do is to rank the subjects from low to high on both variables and then look at the differences (*D*) between the pairs of ranks. The formula is so constructed that *r* will be +1 when the *D*s are all zero; that is, when the two variables are perfectly correlated. When there is a perfect negative correlation the *D*s will tend to be very large, and *r* becomes −1. When there is no relationship between the variables the *D*s will be intermediate in value, and *r* has the value zero.

Spearman's r_s: computation

GENERAL PROCEDURE

I Draw a scattergram.

II Rank the scores on variable *A*, in order, from low to high. Rank the scores on variable *B* in the same way. (Tied ranks are computed by giving each score the arithmetic mean of the ranks that would have been received had there been no ties.)

III Calculate the differences (*D*) between each pair of ranks.

IV Square these differences and sum to obtain the quantity ΣD^2.

V Substitute the value of ΣD^2 and N (the number of subjects) in the following formula and compute r_s:

$$r_s = 1 - \frac{6\Sigma D^2}{N(N^2-1)}$$

VI r_s is then an index of the degree of relationship between the two variables. Its significance may be assessed using table VII, p. 177. The critical value of r_s required for significance at the desired level will depend on (1) N and (2) whether the direction of the correlation was predicted before the study was conducted.

EXAMPLE

The relationship between intelligence and reading speed in a sample of seven 5-year-olds. The investigator predicted a positive relationship between these two variables.

I Scattergram

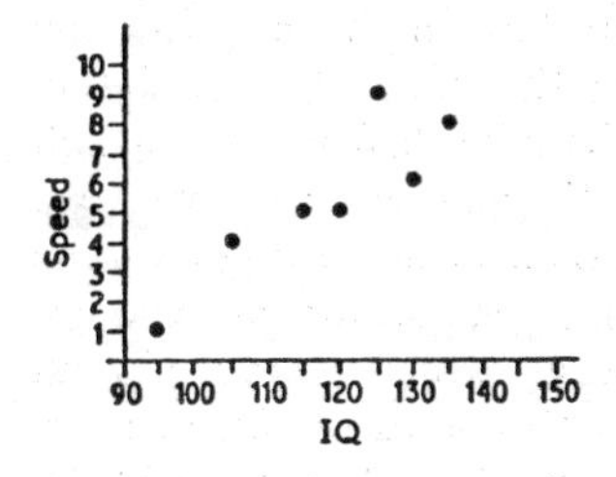

Child	*Speed (words per minute)*	*Intelligence (IQs)*	*Speed rankings*	*IQ rankings*	*D*	D^2
A	8	135	6	7	−1	1
B	6	132	5	6	−1	1
C	10	126	7	5	2	4
D	4	105	2	2	0	0
E	5	120	$3\frac{1}{2}$	4	$-\frac{1}{2}$	$\frac{1}{4}$
F	5	115	$3\frac{1}{2}$	3	$\frac{1}{2}$	$\frac{1}{4}$
G	1	95	1	1	0	0

$\Sigma D^2 = 6\frac{1}{2}$

V $r_s = 1 - \frac{6\Sigma D^2}{N(N^2-1)} = 1 - \frac{6 \times 6\frac{1}{2}}{7 \times 48} = 0{\cdot}88$

VI Using table VII: The critical value of r_s for significance at the $2\frac{1}{2}$ per cent level (one-tailed) is 0·79. As the observed r_s exceeds this value, we can reject the null hypothesis that there is no relationship between reading speed and intelligence.
(Note: if the proportion of ties is substantial a correction factor must be incorporated into the formula for r_s. Details of this are given in Siegel (1956), p. 207.)

The significance of a correlation coefficient

If r is thought of as a descriptive statistic, you may be wondering why it is possible to calculate its significance. Although r describes the relationship between two variables in a sample of pairs of scores, we may still be interested in making inferences about the value of r in the population being sampled. Usually, we wish to know whether an underlying relationship between the two variables, say reading speed and intelligence, can be inferred from the correlation obtained in the sample. Under the null hypothesis the r value for the population is zero. We can test this hypothesis by finding the probability of obtaining a *random* sample from this population with an r value as high as the one obtained. If this probability is 0·05 or less we have a significant correlation, i.e. we can conclude that speed of reading and intelligence are related in the population.

When interpreting the significance of a correlation coefficient we should, of course, remember that associations between variables are not necessarily evidence for cause-and-effect relationships. For example we might obtain a highly significant correlation between height and spelling ability in a sample of school-children. This is unlikely to reflect a direct causal connection between the two variables, but rather the influence of a third variable, age, on both spelling ability and height. This feature of correlational research was discussed in chapter 1.

9

Predicting one variable from another

In some psychological research the objective is simply to discover whether two variables are related to each other. For example, a personality theorist may wish to know whether extraversion is related to the frequency with which people change their jobs, or whether a person's level of neuroticism is correlated with his or her accident record. In this kind of research a correlation either supports or disproves some theoretical view of the world, and that is all that is required.

In contrast, a psychological practitioner will wish to make use of correlational data to predict or influence some aspect of human performance. To do this it is not enough to know that two variables are related, one needs to know the exact form of the relationship in order to make practical use of it. For example, a psychologist working in the field of personnel selection might be interested in the correlation between neuroticism and accident proneness. But he would need to know what levels of neuroticism correspond with various accident rates before he could make use of the relationship. What is needed is a formula or equation that will allow the psychologist to predict a person's accident rate from a knowledge of his or her neuroticism score. The purpose of this chapter is to show how such an equation can be derived,

The topic we are concerned with here is known as *regression* – that is, the prediction of unknown values of one variable from known values of another. By convention the variable we are trying to predict is represented as the Y variable and the variable on which the prediction is based is always the X variable. So in the example above we would be predicting a person's accident rate (Y) from a knowledge of his neuroticism score (X). Thus the problem reduces to finding an equation for Y in terms of X.

The equation of a straight line

Let us immediately simplify matters by restricting the discussion to *linear* relationships of the kind measured by the Pearson r correlation. What does the equation relating X to Y look like if the connection between the variables is linear? We can answer this by plotting some imaginary scattergrams (see figure 17) which show a perfect linear relationship and trying to deduce the appropriate equation for each one. We shall assume that the scattergrams represent children's ages (X) and maximum time-span of attention (Y). As the correlation is perfect in each case a straight line has been drawn through the data points.

Looking first at figure 17(a) we can immediately see the connection betwen X and Y. A 2-year-old can attend for 2 minutes, a 3-year-old for 3 minutes, and so on. So a child's age in years is equivalent to his attention span in minutes. The equation relating age (X) to attention (Y) must therefore be:

$$Y=X \qquad (a)$$

In figure 17(b) we find that a 1-year-old attends for 2 minutes, a 2-year-old for 4 minutes and a 3-year-old for 6 minutes. So attention time is always twice a child's age in years. Thus:

$$Y=2X \qquad (b)$$

Figure 17(c) is also quite straightforward. A 1-year-old attends for 3 minutes, a 2-year-old for 4 minutes and a 3-year-old for 5 minutes. So attention time is 2 minutes greater than age in years.

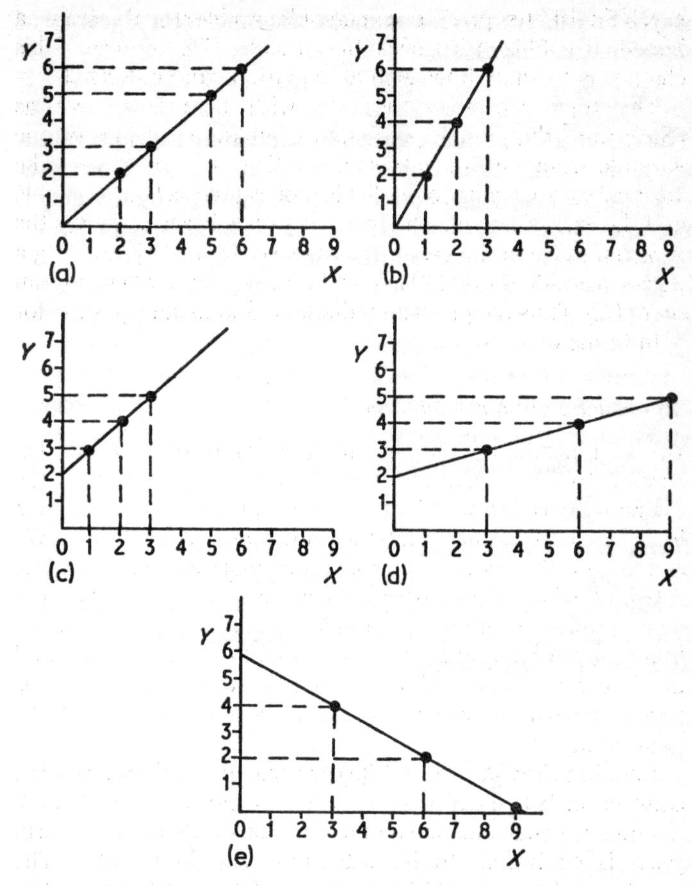

Figure 17 Imaginary scattergrams relating age (X) to attention time (Y)

Thus:

$$Y = X + 2 \qquad (c)$$

Figure 17(d) is slightly more complex. The relations between age and span of attention are: 3 years–3 minutes, 6 years–4 minutes and 9 years–5 minutes. It is clear that attention time goes up by 1 minute for every additional 3 years of age, or equivalently every extra year of age produces $\frac{1}{3}$ minute rise in attention. But Y is not simply $\frac{1}{3}X$, because even when X is 0, Y

still has a value of 2. A few minutes' trial-and-error algebra will show that in this case:

$$Y = \tfrac{1}{3}X + 2 \qquad (d)$$

You can check that this is correct by substituting various values for X in the equation. If X is replaced by 3 years, Y becomes $(\frac{1}{3} \times 3) + 2 = 3$, which is correct. If X is replaced by 6 years, Y becomes $(\frac{1}{3} \times 6) + 2 = 4$, which also fits the original data. So the equation must be a correct description of figure 17(d).

Finally, we turn to figure 17(c) which shows a negative relationship between age and attention – the older the child, the shorter his or her span of attention. Specifically a 3-year-old has 4 minutes, a 6-year-old has 2 minutes and a 9-year-old has 0 minutes! So attention span is declining by 2 minutes every 3 years, or by $\frac{2}{3}$ minute per year. Again a little experimentation will show that the correct equation is:

$$Y = -\tfrac{2}{3}X + 6 \qquad (e)$$

If you wish to prove this is correct, substitute the original values of X and check whether the right values of Y are generated.

Now what have we learned about the equation of a straight line? The first point to note is that all the equations conform to a standard pattern, namely:

$$Y = bX + a \qquad (1)$$

where a and b are constants. Sometimes a is 0 and does not appear (as in figure 17(a)). Sometimes b is 1 and is therefore not obvious (as in figure 17(c)). But any equation of a straight line will conform to the general format of equation (1).

By comparing each equation with its graph we can also see that a and b have meanings in terms of the features of figure 17. In figures 17(a) and (b) a is 0 and the lines pass through the origin. In figures 17(c) and (d) a is 2 and the lines pass through the Y axis at $Y=2$. In figure 17(e) a is 6 and the line passes through the Y axis at $Y=6$. For all straight line equations it can be shown that a corresponds to the value of Y where the line crosses the Y axis, i.e. the intercept.

By a similar process we can learn the meaning of b. In figures 17(a) and (c) b is 1 and the lines increase by 1 unit of Y for every 1 unit increase in X. In figure 17(b) b is 2 and the line rises 2 units of Y for every 1 unit increase in X. In figure 17(d) b is $\frac{1}{3}$ and the line rises $\frac{1}{3}$ units of Y for every unit increase in X. And in figure 17(e) b is $-\frac{2}{3}$ and the line *falls* by $\frac{2}{3}$ units of Y for every unit increase in X. All this shows that b *represents the gradient or slope of the graph*, i.e. the number of units of Y by which the line rises or falls per unit increase in X.

The least squares regression line

We have now established the general form of the equation of a straight line. The equation is, in effect, a formula for calculating the value of Y for any given value of X. This is exactly what is needed for the purposes of regression, since regression involves predicting a subject's score on Y given that you know his score on X.

If all samples of data exhibited the perfect correlations shown in figure 17, the process of regression would be remarkably simple. We would just have to draw the scattergram, rule in the single line going through all the data points, measure the gradient and intercept (b and a) and write out the equation $Y=bX+a$. This equation would predict *perfectly* the value of Y for any conceivable value of X.

However the typical correlation observed in psychology is far from perfect, and it will produce a scattergram more like the example shown in figure 18. The problem then is to find the best fitting line going through this scatter of points; that is the line which would involve the smallest errors if we used it to predict Y from X.

There are, in fact, several criteria that might be used to define the line of best fit. It might be argued that the line which

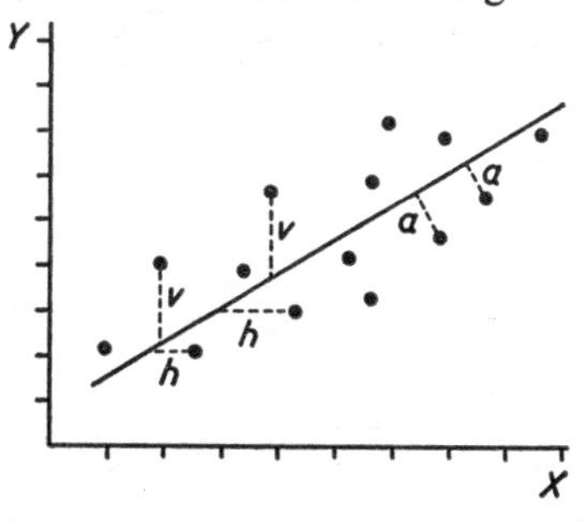

Figure 18 Typical scattergram showing three types of deviation from the regression line

minimizes the horizontal distances between the points and itself (i.e. the *hs* is figure 18) was the best fit. Or perhaps we might try to find the line which minimizes the *shortest* distances between each data point and itself (i.e. the *as*). Or should we minimize the vertical deviations – the *vs*? Given that our aim is to predict Y as accurately as possible, we make use of the third criterion of what constitutes the best fit. More precisely, we define the regression line as *that line which minimizes the squared deviations between the points and the line measured in the Y direction*; i.e. the line that minimizes Σv^2. This line is known as the least squares regression line.

Finding the equation of the regression line

With the scatter of points shown in figure 18 it is obviously not possible to draw in the best fitting line by eye. Fortunately there are standard formulae which determine the values of a and b for any given set of data. Once a and b have been determined they can be substituted in the general equation $Y = bX + a$ to give the regression equation for predicting Y from X.

GENERAL PROCEDURE

I Draw a scattergram. This will indicate whether the relationship is approximately linear and will give you a rough idea – by looking at the slope and intercept of the points – what kind of equation to expect. (If the relationship is obviously non-linear the regression equation will be virtually useless for prediction.)

II Set out the two measures for each subject as follows, being sure to label the predictor variable X and the variable to be predicted Y:

	X	Y	XY	X^2
S_1	—	—		
S_2	—	—		
S_3	—	—		
•	•	•		
•	•	•		
•	•	•		
•	•	•		
S_N	—	—		
	ΣX	ΣY	ΣXY	ΣX^2

(Note: we do *not* need to calculate the Y^2 values to get the regression equation.)

III Fill in the rest of the table shown in II. The XY column contains the products of each subject's X and Y scores. The X^2 column contains the squares of each subject's X scores.

IV Find the totals of the entries in each column, i.e. ΣX, ΣY, ΣXY, ΣX^2.

V Substitute these values in the formulae for b and a:

$$b = \frac{N\Sigma XY - (\Sigma X)(\Sigma Y)}{N\Sigma X^2 - (\Sigma X)^2}$$

$$a = \frac{\Sigma Y}{N} - b\frac{\Sigma X}{N}$$

(*Note: the formula for a* makes use of the value obtained for b from the previous formula.)

VI The regression equation for predicting Y from X is then given by substituting a and b into:

$Y = bX + a$

EXAMPLE

A psychologist wishes to develop an equation to predict a child's span of attention on the basis of the child's age. He obtains the following pairs of observations using a sample of ten children.

	S_1	S_2	S_3	S_4	S_5	S_6	S_7	S_8	S_9	S_{10}
Age (in years)	3	7	5	4	8	3	9	4	6	11
Attention span (minutes)	6	11	8	7	13	5	15	7	10	18

I Scattergram

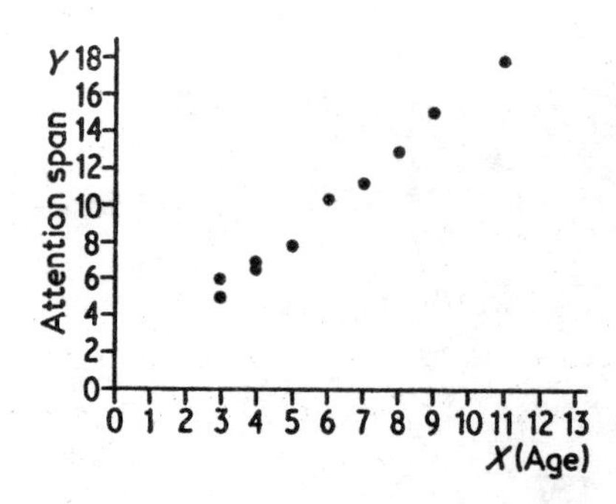

It is clear from the scattergram that a strong linear relationship exists between age and attention span. The gradient of the regression line will be approximately 1·5 (attention span rises by about 13 minutes over an age range of 8 years, so the gradient is about 13/8 or $>1{\cdot}5$). The intercept on the Y axis appears to be about 1 (this is estimated by placing a ruler through the data points and extending the approximate 'regression line' back to the Y axis). So a quick inspection leads us to expect a regression line something like: $Y=1{\cdot}5X+1$. If the final outcome is dramatically different from this estimate we would suspect a mistake in the calculations.

II and III

	Age (years) X	Attention (minutes) Y	XY	X^2
S_1	3	6	18	9
S_2	7	11	77	49
S_3	5	8	40	25
S_4	4	7	28	16
S_5	8	13	104	64
S_6	3	5	15	9
S_7	9	15	135	81
S_8	4	7	28	16
S_9	6	10	60	36
S_{10}	11	18	198	121

IV $\Sigma X=60 \quad \Sigma Y=100 \quad \Sigma XY=703 \quad \Sigma X^2=426$

V $$b=\frac{N\Sigma XY-(\Sigma X)(\Sigma Y)}{N\Sigma X^2-(\Sigma X)^2}=\frac{10\times 703-60\times 100}{10\times 426-60\times 60}$$

$$=\frac{7030-6000}{4260-3600}=1{\cdot}56$$

$$a=\frac{\Sigma Y}{N}-b\frac{\Sigma X}{N}=\frac{100}{10}-1{\cdot}56\times\frac{60}{10}$$

$$=10-1{\cdot}56\times 6=0{\cdot}64$$

VI Hence the regression equation for predicting attention span given a child's age is:

$$Y = 1{\cdot}56X + 0{\cdot}64$$

Thus a 5-year-old, for example, would be expected to have a span of attention of:

$$Y = 1{\cdot}56 \times 5 + 0{\cdot}64 = 8{\cdot}44 \text{ minutes}$$

We note that the final equation is similar to the estimated equation of the regression line based on inspection of the scattergram.

The use of the regression line

This chapter only provides a simple introduction to the topic of linear regression. The least squares equation can be used to predict one variable from another when the relationship is linear and reasonably strong. If the first limitation is broken, a non-linear regression technique must be employed. If the relationship between X and Y is a weak one, it may be that predictability can be improved by using two or more variables as the basis for prediction. Indeed, in most practical applications you will find that behaviour can only be predicted well by taking account of many different variables. Think for a moment of the number of factors that influence your own performance, say, in an examination. Predictions based on several variables are covered by the topic of *multiple regression.* This area is fully discussed in the companion text *Multivariate Design and Statistics* (Miller, forthcoming).

10

Experimental design and beyond

In the earlier chapters of this book we have followed through various aspects of the design and analysis of simple experiments. In this final chapter we shall provide an overview of the sequence of decisions which need to be made, and elaborate on those which have not yet been discussed. We shall also emphasize the interconnections between some of the stages. In the final section some thought will be given to the question of generalization beyond the specific findings of a particular study.

An overview of experimental design

There are a number of ways one could set out the steps involved in the design and analysis of experiments. The format used here agrees with that adopted by Gardiner and Kaminska (1975), in their practical examples of experimental design in psychology.

(1) Conceptualization of the problem

The first step in designing an experiment was blithely described in chapter 2 thus: 'We begin with a prediction that we are interested in testing'. It would be more accurate to say that we *end* the first stage of scientific inquiry with a prediction that we are interested in testing. A prediction is a specific statement about the relationship between two variables which is the *outcome* of earlier thinking of a more general and disorganized kind. We know surprisingly little about the processes which underly this kind of thinking. But certainly the formulation of predictions is a more creative and intuitive endeavour than we are often led to believe in journal articles and scientific reports. Very few psychological hypotheses are actually formulated by direct deductions from some more general theory. They must surely arise from some kind of interaction between the experimenter's intuitions, theoretical ideas and factual knowledge. In contrast to the more formal aspects of experimental design, the generation of a research problem defies logical analysis, and there are certainly no guidelines for the formulation of fruitful or successful approaches.

Nevertheless we can say that the hypothesis arising out of this activity must be testable, that is, we must be able to obtain some factual evidence which has the potential to support, or refute, the theory being tested. Otherwise the problem falls outside the realm of scientific inquiry. The prediction is a guarantee of testability. By requiring a statement of the predicted relationship between two variables, we ensure that the conceptual activities of the experimenter produce something that can be evaluated using scientific methods.

(2) Experimental design

The design of an experiment is the general plan which is to be used in testing a given prediction. This plan specifies the way in which the relevant data are to be collected. Many of the important points were discussed in chapter 1. These will not be summarized here, but certain other points will be discussed.

(A) HOW MANY CONDITIONS?

Once a prediction has been framed the first step is to decide on the number of levels of the independent variable. We have assumed in this book that you will normally be comparing just two conditions, which makes life easier from the statistical point of view. But there are obvious advantages to taking several levels into consideration especially if the independent variable is of a quantitative nature, such as noise level or drug dosage. In such cases we may be interested in knowing the functional relationship between the independent and dependent variables. If this relationship is a complex one, such as the U-shaped function depicted in figure 16(f) (p. 134) the information obtained from just two experimental conditions will tell us virtually nothing about the intervening sections of the curve. Indeed, if we were unlucky in the choice of values for the independent variable we might be misled into thinking that there was no relationship at all. In a k-sample design, even where k is only three, these risks are substantially reduced. But on the other hand the practical problems of time, money and the recruitment of extra subjects must be set against the extra precision inherent in these designs.

If the independent variable is qualitative in nature – such as 'training method' or 'concrete versus abstract nouns' – then the arguments for choosing several different levels are obviously inappropriate. In such cases the levels have been selected because of their intrinsic interest to the experimenter and not as a means of plotting out the functional relationship between the two variables.

(B) THE ALLOCATION OF SUBJECTS TO CONDITIONS

The second step in setting out the design of the experiment concerns the choice between the three methods of allocating subjects to conditions – repeated-measures, matched-subjects and independent-groups designs. The relative effectiveness of these designs in the control of subject variability was discussed quite fully in chapter 1. We might add here, however, that considerations *other than* control efficiency will creep into the final choice between them. Thus a decision to study the effects of many different levels of the independent variable may cause us to adopt a non-optimal design, say the independent groups design, because of the difficulty of obtaining subjects for a long enough time to complete all k conditions in the repeated measures design.

Another consideration in the choice of design is the question of the availability of appropriate statistical techniques. With the limited repertoire of two-group designs included in this book it is unlikely that you could choose a design that was incapable of being analysed. But the risk of this happening increases in proportion to the ambitiousness of your experiments. It is therefore essential that you plan the statistical analysis *at the design stage* of the experiment.

(C) THE SUBJECTS

There are two decisions to be made regarding subjects. First we wish to know how many subjects should be recruited in order to be reasonably confident of detecting the experimental effect, if there is one. Secondly we need to consider how the subjects are to be selected.

Suppose, for a moment, that we know the independent variable is having an effect on the dependent variable. Equivalently, we could say that we know two hypothetical populations have different means. What factors will influence the chance of our getting significance from a statistical test based on samples from these populations? Fairly obviously the separation of the population means will be relevant. The greater the difference, the more likely we are to get significance. A second factor is the variability in the two populations; the greater the variability, the lower the chance of significance. As we learned in chapter 1, this variability will be determined in large part by the design of the experiment. A third factor is the size of the two samples: the larger the samples, the greater the chance of detecting the underlying difference in the populations. Unfortunately we are very unlikely to know, before the experiment, what value to place on the variability of the scores, or the probable difference in population means. Thus we cannot actually calculate the sample sizes needed to stand a good chance of detecting significance. All we can say is that the prospects grow better as the sample is increased. In practical terms this normally means that we should run as many subjects as our time and resources allow. At least this is so until we have established from past research the sort of distribution of scores that are likely to arise. With this knowledge one can develop a 'feel' for the number of subjects needed to produce significant results. A 'pilot' study can be immensely useful in this respect.

A second point which must be decided is the method of selecting subjects for the experiment. In theoretical terms we should select our subjects randomly from the population of people or animals to which we intend to generalize our experimental findings. In practice, the choice of subjects is determined by the availability of particular individuals and perhaps also by decisions to reduce subject variability by holding a given characteristic constant. Hence we purchase practical *convenience* and increased *precision* at the expense of *random sampling* from the broad population of interest. This crucial decision influences our freedom to generalize from the experiment to a wider context, as will be discussed in the final section of the book.

(D) THE CONTROL OF SITUATIONAL VARIABLES

Another important aspect of experimental design is the strategy used to control environmental factors, such as noise, which might possibly contaminate the experimental effect we are interested in. The relevant methods are discussed in chapter 1. We might note here, however, that strict control in the form of holding particular variables constant can be overdone. To be sure, this method of control reduces random variations in the data, which is desirable, but if too many variables are controlled in this way the experiment becomes unduly 'pure' – almost over-sensitive to the effects of the independent variable. There is something to be said for the view that an experimental effect should be robust enough to emerge over and above the random effects that operate in real life. If an experiment is very rigorously controlled we simply cannot know how robust the findings are. This is a matter of some importance when the research is meant to inform practical decision-making.

A second drawback of rigorous control is discussed in the final section.

(3) Operationalizing the experiment

The basic experimental design must be translated into a concrete specification of the experiment. The nature of these procedural details is illustrated at the beginning of chapter 2. One important decision which may be made at this stage relates to the measurement of the independent variable. If the prediction specifies the dependent variable fairly precisely, our decision at this stage may simply concern the number of individual responses which will be combined to form the measure of performance. Thus, if the dependent variable is reaction time, the decision might be to take the mean of 100 reaction times as an index of the subject's performance in each condition. However, if the dependent variable mentioned in the prediction is something like 'learning', we shall have to give considerable attention to the choice between such measures as 'trials to criterion', 'speed of performance', 'error rate' and so forth. The nature of the theory underlying the prediction will be a major influence on this choice, as will more practical considerations such as the time available to test the subjects. In addition we should be concerned with the reliability, validity, sensitivity and statistical characteristics of the measure that is to be selected. *Reliability* refers to the consistency of the measurement; that is, the extent to which the measure would remain constant for any particular subject if he or she were repeatedly tested under identical conditions. Lack of reliability in the measurement technique will simply add to the random effects in the data, further reducing the clarity of the experimental effect. We can often improve the reliability of a measure by taking the mean of several independent observations on the same subject. In this way any 'freak' circumstances which might have influenced one observation will tend to balance out over the set. Thus one reaction time is a highly unreliable measure of a subject's characteristic speed of responding, whereas the mean of 100 reaction times is a remarkably stable index of performance.

Validity refers to the correspondence between the operational procedures used in measurement and the theoretical construct which is supposedly being measured. Thus the measurement of intelligence on the basis of 'head size' would be perfectly reliable, but totally lacking in validity. We can measure head size consistently, but it simply does not reflect intelligence. A test of reasoning would be more valid. When the dependent variable is something like 'creativity' or 'aggressiveness' the problems of measurement validity may be quite acute. In these cases the idea of *construct validity* is important. This involves the judgement of the validity of a measure on the basis of many interrelated experimental findings. If a series of predictions are confirmed using a particular measure of creativity then the underlying theory *and* the validity of the measure gain credence simultaneously. This approach is necessary when a construct has no obvious independent criterion against which its measurement may be validated. Of course, when our predictions concern directly observable characteristics such as reaction time or pupil dilation, the problem of establishing construct validity does not arise.

The *sensitivity* of a variable refers to the extent to which it changes in response to changes in the independent variable. Thus we might find that the *skill* in manipulating a vehicle was not impaired under certain levels of alcohol consumption, whereas the tendency of drivers to take risks was increased. Other things being equal, one might then adopt the risk-taking measure as a criterion of performance in future studies of drinking and driving.

Finally, we should consider the level of measurement (see p. 62) and the form of the distribution of all potential response measures. Naturally those which satisfy the requirements for the more powerful, parametric techniques of analysis are to be preferred.

(4) Analysis and interpretation of results

In this book we have focused on the statistical analysis of results, leading to inferences concerning the reliability of the difference between groups of scores. There is a grave danger that statistical significance may blind the experimenter to possible weaknesses of design and conceptualization which underly the numerical results. The question to be answered at the end of an experiment is *not* – what level of significance was obtained? Rather we should ask the question – to what extent do these results confirm the original prediction and throw light on the theoretical notions which gave rise to that prediction? The point we wish to emphasize here is that many considerations external to the statistical analysis will determine the practical and theoretical significance of the results. These considerations include: the adequacy of the design; the magnitude of the experimental effect (as distinct from its purely statistical significance); the nature of the subject population; the extent to which the naivety of the subjects was maintained; the introspective reports of the subjects; the possibility of the experimenter 'inducing' results which confirm his predictions, and so forth.

Generalizing from experiments

Many experiments end with a high significance level and a smiling experimenter. But what exactly does a significant result tell us about the world at large? About human behaviour outside the laboratory? Or even about other people who might have been tested inside the laboratory? These are questions concerning our ability to generalize from experimental results. The issues raised are controversial and a full discussion would be impossible within the confines of this book. Nevertheless, there are a few basic points which should be made.

Strictly speaking, there is only one basis in scientific method for generalizing outside of the specific circumstances in which the experiment takes place. This basis is *random sampling.* If we select the subjects to be used in an experiment at random from some population of interest, then it is legitimate to generalize our findings back to that population of people. But the requirement of random sampling does not apply only to populations of people. Our findings are equally tied to the physical context of the experiment. If we want to say that variable *A* influences variable *B* generally – that is, in various places, at various times, in various climates, using various experimenters, etc. – then, as far as statistical inference is concerned, we must randomly sample these various times, places, experimenters, and so on. Now although the sampling of subject populations may sometimes be feasible, it is patently impossible to sample these other aspects of the experimental environment. Does this mean that our findings are rigidly tied to the particular circumstances in which our experiment took place? The answer is both yes and no. As far as statistical inference is concerned, the answer must be yes. But we are, of course, free to make discretionary judgements outside of the strict confines of scientific method, i.e. *non*-statistical inferences. If it seems to us that a particular feature of the subject's behaviour is unlikely to be influenced by a change of experimenter, temperature, or whatever, then we shall treat our results as though they applied in these different circumstances. On the other hand, if a result does seem, on intuitive or other bases, to be dependent on some circumstance of the experiment – say a pretty experimenter, or an unusually hot day – then we should tread much more warily. The point is, then, that the extent to which particular findings are held to be generally applicable is a matter for you and the scientific community to decide, on the basis of what seems likely from our knowledge and intuitions about behaviour, but *not* on the basis of any formal procedures of inference, which can only be used when random sampling from the population of interest has taken place.

Perhaps the most critical restriction on our ability to generalize comes from the fact that the vast majority of psychological experimentation makes use of '*volunteers*' drawn from very specific populations such as other experimenters, psychology students, or third-year civil engineering students whose grants have run out! Nobody could possibly claim that such groups approximate to *random* samples from any population, certainly *not* from any population of general relevance to mankind. So we cannot make statistical inferences, and we have to be especially careful about making non-statistical inferences to 'the larger population'. We might feel reasonably happy about extending some findings, say in the field of physiological psychology, but our conclusions about human intellectual functioning may be quite erroneous if applied uncritically to non-student populations.

Unfortunately there is an aspect of statistics which tends to obscure the problem. You will appreciate by now the central importance of the concepts of sample and population in statistical inference. The typical statistical test ends with a statement of the form: 'This result shows that the two samples of scores come from populations with different means.' What could be better designed to suggest to you, and the reader, that you have discovered something which may be generalized to some larger population? Indeed many statistics texts encourage you to think this is so. For example, statistical inference is often introduced as a topic which will 'allow you to generalize the specific findings of your experiment to larger populations'. This, of course, is true only if the experimental scores really are random samples from existing populations. But in most experiments this is not the case. Our samples are typical of nobody but themselves. And the 'populations' of statistical inference are not populations of people, but purely *imaginary*, conceptual populations – populations of hypothetical scores which are used in statistical *thinking* but which have no relevance to any physical entity outside of the experiment itself.

Using other methods (see, for example, Edgington, 1969) it is possible to calculate significance levels without even using the theoretical notions of sample and population. If these methods were in general use we might be less likely to confuse inferences about the effects of the independent variable, which are legitimate products of statistical testing, with inferences about 'larger populations', which are not.

Although the only scientific justification for generalization is properly organized random sampling from the populations of interest, there is a sort of spurious sampling which takes place anyway. For example, if you choose to allow, say, temperature to vary during your experiment there is a sense in which you have sampled different levels of this variable. This 'sampling' will make it easier for you to claim generality for your results, but it will simultaneously prejudice your chances of gaining significance. As we have said many times, the more random variation in each group of scores, the less likely it is that the effects of the independent variable will emerge above the 'noise'. When you consider that there are vast numbers of irrelevant variables that could either be rigorously controlled, or allowed to vary randomly, a difficult decision has to be made. At one extreme we could hold all the relevant variables we can manage constant – yielding a sensitive design but a highly unrealistic base from which to generalize – and at the other we could allow everything to vary randomly – yielding a very insensitive design, but a very strong base from which to generalize (always assuming that significance is obtained). This choice exemplifies an important feature of the field of experimental design: There is rarely a single, ideal solution to a design problem. The most reliable measure may involve the greatest inconvenience for the experimenter. The most sensitive design may require assumptions about the data which cannot be substantiated. Experimental design involves the weighing of such factors and the choice between the alternatives. The rules by which we can reach these decisions will obviously depend on the circumstances of each study. We can, however, identify the factors which should influence our decision making, and this has been the aim of much of this book. No doubt you will find these issues somewhat academic in the early stages, but they should become relevant, and even exciting, as soon as you become involved in your first research project. And you will gradually find that your own experience leads you towards the optimal choices.

Table A.2 Frequency distribution of the test scores of 100 students

Score	*Frequency*
42	1
43	2
44	0
45	4
46	5
47	7
48	12
49	14
50	20
51	14
52	12
53	6
54	3
	$N=100$

construct the frequency distribution shown in table A.2, and then compute the mean (and other statistics such as the variance) from the tabulated data.

First we shall derive the appropriate formula for use with a frequency distribution. As usual, the mean will be defined as the sum of all the scores divided by the total number of scores. Looking at table A.2 we can see that the sum of all the scores will be given by:

$$(42\times 1)+(43\times 2)+(44\times 0)\ldots\ldots\ldots(54\times 3) \qquad (A)$$

(This is just another way of saying that the total of the scores is given by $42+43+43+45+45+45$ and so on.) In words, we are simply multiplying each score by the number of times it occurs and then adding all these products together.

How can we express this in symbols? If x stands for any score in the table and f stands for its frequency of occurrence then fx stands for the product of the score times its frequency. Now we want to add all these products together as shown in the expression (A) above. We can express this in symbols by Σfx, i.e.

multiply each score by its frequency and add all the products together.

Having obtained the sum of all the scores, we simply have to divide by the number of scores, N. Hence the formula for the mean of data presented in a frequency distribution is:

$$\bar{X} = \frac{\Sigma fx}{N}$$

The use of this formula is illustrated in table A.3. If the data had been grouped into classes, as in table 8, we would proceed in exactly the same way, but using the midpoints of each class as the x values.

Table A.3 Computation of the mean from a frequency distribution of 100 test scores

Score x	*Frequency* f	*Score × frequency* fx
42	1	42
43	2	86
44	0	0
45	4	180
46	5	230
47	7	329
48	12	576
49	14	686
50	20	1000
51	14	714
52	12	624
53	6	318
54	3	162
	$N = 100$	$\Sigma fx = 4947$

$$\bar{X} = \frac{\Sigma fx}{N} = \frac{4947}{100} = 49{\cdot}47$$

(Note: We have used the symbol x to stand for each possible score, rather than X which was used previously. This is because we are now talking about all the *possible values* that a score could take, and not all the *actual scores*. Thus in the data of table A.3 there are thirteen values of x, including 44, which is a *possible value* even though it doesn't actually occur. On the other hand, there are 100 values of X – that is, all the actual scores. Naturally if every value of x occurred just once then x would have the same meaning as X.)

The mean: method II

CODING SCORES FOR COMPUTATION

Looking at table A.3 it can be seen that even with this method of computation we still have to do some rather complicated arithmetic. There is yet a further simplification we can introduce to alleviate much of the labour, by subtracting a constant from each value of x, calculating the mean using the new values of x (usually called x') and then adding on the constant again at the end. We can subtract any constant we like, but the best value to choose is one that seems fairly close to the mean, say 50 in the present example. This allows us to work with much smaller numbers, some of which will be negative and will therefore 'cancel out' with the positive entries. If we represent the constant by the letter c, then the formula for calculating the mean becomes:

$$\bar{X} = \frac{\Sigma fx'}{N} + c$$

The use of this formula is illustrated in table A.4. Note that it produces the same result as the previous method but involves much simpler computations. This is useful if you are working without a desk calculator, but otherwise the labour of *coding* the data is hardly offset by the time saved in computing.

The median

Once the data are arranged in the form of a frequency distribution the median can be obtained fairly easily. First we decide which is the middle position in the series of N scores. When $N = 100$ this will fall between the 50th and 51st scores in the order from lowest to highest. We then move down the column of frequencies until we reach a total frequency of 50 and

Table A.4 Computation of the mean from a frequency distribution of 100 test scores using coded data

Score x	*Frequency* f	*Score* − 50 x'	*Frequency* × *coded score* fx'
42	1	−8	− 8
43	2	−7	−14
44	0	−6	0
45	4	−5	−20
46	5	−4	−20
47	7	−3	−21
48	12	−2	−24
49	14	−1	−14
50	20	0	0
51	14	1	14
52	12	2	24
53	6	3	18
54	3	4	12
	$N=100$		$\Sigma fx' = -53$

$$\bar{X} = \frac{\Sigma fx'}{N} + c = \frac{-53}{100} + 50 = -0{\cdot}53 + 50 = 49{\cdot}47$$

read off the score corresponding to this point. We also note the score corresponding to the 51st observation. The point halfway between the 50th and 51st scores will be the median.

Looking down the frequency distribution in table A.2 we find that the scores between 42 and 49 account for the lowest 45 observations. The score of 50 accounts for the next 20 observations, including of course the 50th and 51st items. Thus the median score has a value of 50.

A more sensitive measure of the median can be obtained by treating the score of 50 as though it were a class of scores spread between 49·5 and 50·5. We can then locate the 'true' median within this class interval. Since 45 per cent of the scores are already accounted for, we wish to move into the interval between 49·5 and 50·5 to the point where a further 5 per cent of the scores have been passed. As 20 per cent of all the scores fall into this interval we must move exactly one-quarter of the way through it to cover an extra 5 per cent of the scores. Thus the median is $49{\cdot}5+\frac{1}{4}\times 1=49{\cdot}75$. For most purposes the simpler method described above provides a good enough approximation to the median.

The mode

The mode is defined as the most frequently occurring value in a set of scores. Obviously this value can be read directly from the frequency distribution. Thus the mode of the data in table A.2 is 50.

(Note: the mean, median and mode have very similar values for the distribution of scores considered in this section. This is because the distribution is almost perfectly symmetrical in shape; see p. 31.)

Appendix 2: calculating the variance and standard deviation from a frequency distribution

Method I

Consider again the raw data given in table A.1 (p. 162). The basic formula for calculating the variance $(\Sigma X^2/N - \bar{X}^2)$ would require us to square each score and then find the sum of these squares. However, since many scores occur several times, it would be wasteful to repeatedly square and add the same figure. Using a frequency distribution we can square each *possible* score, x, just once, and then multiply by the number of times x occurs in the data, that is, f. The formula for the variance then becomes:

$$S^2 = \frac{\Sigma fx^2}{N} = \bar{X}$$

The use of this formula to find the variance (and standard deviation) of the 100 test scores is demonstrated in table A.5. Note that the mean is also calculated from the formula appropriate to frequency distribution.

Table A.5 Computation of the variance and standard deviation of 100 test scores based on a frequency distribution

Score x	*Frequency* f	*Frequency × score* fx	*Frequency × score*^{2} fx^2
42	1	42	1 764
43	2	86	3 698
44	0	0	0
45	4	180	8 100
46	5	230	10 580
47	7	329	15 463
48	12	576	27 648
49	14	686	33 614
50	20	1000	50 000
51	14	714	36 414
52	12	624	32 448
53	6	318	16 854
54	3	162	8 748
	$N = 100$	$\Sigma fx = 4947$	$\Sigma fx^2 = 245\,331$

Mean

$$\bar{X} = \frac{\Sigma fx}{N} = \frac{4947}{100} = 49{\cdot}47$$

Variance

$$S^2 = \frac{\Sigma fx^2}{N} - \bar{X}^2$$

$$= \frac{245331}{100} - 49{\cdot}47^2$$

$$= 2453{\cdot}31 - 2447{\cdot}281$$

$$= 6{\cdot}029$$

Standard deviation

$$S = \sqrt{6{\cdot}029} = 2{\cdot}46$$

Method II

Coding scores for computation

As we did with the mean, it is possible to reduce the arithmetical labour involved in a computation by subtracting a constant from every score in the distribution. In the case of the mean we had to add this constant back on again at the end of the calculation. This is an obvious step; if we subtract 50 from every score the mean of the 'new' scores will clearly be 50 less than the mean of the original data. But in the case of the variance there is no need to add back the constant at the end of the calculation. The reason is, of course, that the variance is a measure of *spread*, and the spread in a set of score has nothing to do with their absolute values; the variability of the scores 1, 2, 3, will be exactly the same as the variability of the scores 1001, 1002, 1003. It is the *differences* between the scores that determines spread, so that the addition or subtraction of any figure from *all* the scores will not change the value of the variance (or any other measure of dispersion).

Armed with this knowledge we can now go ahead and calculate the variance of the 100 test scores using data which have been coded in a more convenient form. As with the mean, the greatest simplification will occur if we subtract a constant that seems fairly close to the mean – say 50 in the present case. The appropriate calculations are demonstrated in table A.6.

Do not forget, when using this method, that although the variance is unchanged by subtracting a constant, the mean is not. Thus the mean of the coded data–which is used in the process of finding the variance–is not the mean of the original data. To make this clear we shall refer to it as $\bar{X}'$. Hence the formula for the variance of coded data is:

$$S^2 = \frac{\Sigma f x'^2}{N} - \bar{X}'^2$$

Table A.6 Computation of variance and standard deviation of 100 test scores using a coding procedure

Score x	*Frequency* f	*Score − 50* x'	*Frequency × coded score* fx'	*Frequency × coded score*^{2} fx'^2
42	1	−8	−8	64
43	2	−7	−14	98
44	0	−6	0	0
45	4	−5	−20	100
46	5	−4	−20	80
47	7	−3	−21	63
48	12	−2	−24	48
49	14	−1	−14	14
50	20	0	0	0
51	14	1	14	14
52	12	2	24	48
53	6	3	18	54
54	3	4	12	48
	$N=100$		$\Sigma fx' = -53$	$\Sigma fx'^2 = 631$

Mean of coded scores $\bar{X}' = \dfrac{\Sigma fx'}{N} = \dfrac{-53}{100} = -0{\cdot}53$

Variance $S^2 = \dfrac{\Sigma fx'^2}{N} - \bar{X}'^2 = \dfrac{631}{100} - (-0{\cdot}53)^2 = 6{\cdot}31 + 0{\cdot}281 = 6{\cdot}029$

Standard deviation $S = \sqrt{6{\cdot}029} = 2{\cdot}46$

Appendix 3: statistical tables

Table I The normal distribution

Proportion of total area under the normal curve which is beyond any given Z score. Table is appropriate for a *one-tailed test.* (For a two-tailed test the probabilities should be doubled.)

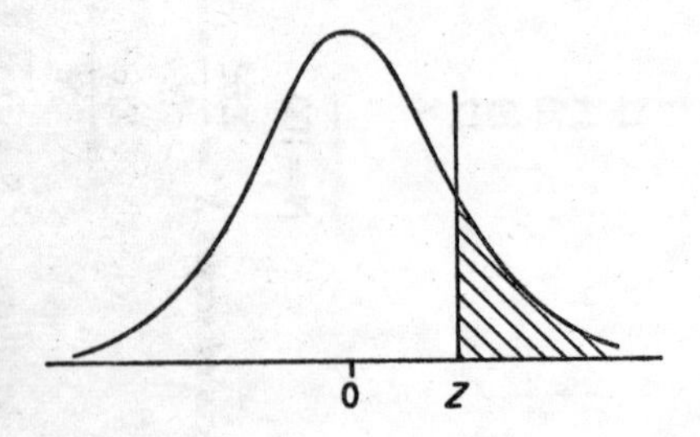

The left-hand margin gives values of Z to one decimal place.
The top row gives value of Z to the second decimal place.

Z	·00	·01	·02	·03	·04	·05	·06	·07	·08	·09
·0	·5000	·4960	·4920	·4880	·4840	·4801	·4761	·4721	·4681	·4641
·1	·4602	·4562	·4522	·4483	·4443	·4404	·4364	·4325	·4286	·4247
·2	·4207	·4168	·4129	·4090	·4052	·4013	·3974	·3936	·3897	·3859
·3	·3821	·3783	·3745	·3707	·3669	·3632	·3594	·3557	·3520	·3483
·4	·3446	·3409	·3372	·3336	·3300	·3264	·3228	·3192	·3156	·3121
·5	·3085	·3050	·3015	·2981	·2946	·2912	·2877	·2843	·2810	·2776
·6	·2743	·2709	·2676	·2643	·2611	·2578	·2546	·2514	·2483	·2451
·7	·2420	·2389	·2358	·2327	·2296	·2266	·2236	·2206	·2177	·2148
·8	·2119	·2090	·2061	·2033	·2005	·1977	·1949	·1922	·1894	·1867
·9	·1814	·1841	·1788	·1762	·1736	·1711	·1685	·1660	·1635	·1611
1·0	·1587	·1562	·1539	·1515	·1492	·1469	·1446	·1423	·1401	·1379
1·1	·1357	·1335	·1314	·1292	·1271	·1251	·1230	·1210	·1190	·1170
1·2	·1151	·1131	·1112	·1093	·1075	·1056	·1038	·1020	·1003	·0985
1·3	·0968	·0951	·0934	·0918	·0901	·0885	·0869	·0853	·0838	·0823
1·4	·0808	·0793	·0778	·0764	·0749	·0735	·0721	·0708	·0694	·0681
1·5	·0668	·0655	·0643	·0630	·0618	·0606	·0594	·0582	·0571	·0559
1·6	·0548	·0537	·0526	·0516	·0505	·0495	·0485	·0475	·0465	·0455
1·7	·0446	·0436	·0427	·0418	·0409	·0401	·0392	·0384	·0375	·0367
1·8	·0359	·0351	·0344	·0336	·0329	·0322	·0314	·0307	·0301	·0294
1·9	·0287	·0281	·0274	·0268	·0262	·0256	·0250	·0244	·0239	·0233
2·0	·0228	·0222	·0217	·0212	·0207	·0202	·0197	·0192	·0188	·0183
2·1	·0179	·0174	·0170	·0166	·0162	·0158	·0154	·0150	·0146	·0143
2·2	·0139	·0136	·0132	·0129	·0125	·0122	·0119	·0116	·0113	·0110
2·3	·0107	·0104	·0102	·0099	·0096	·0094	·0091	·0089	·0087	·0084
2·4	·0082	·0080	·0078	·0075	·0073	·0071	·0069	·0068	·0066	·0064
2·5	·0062	·0060	·0059	·0057	·0055	·0054	·0052	·0051	·0049	·0048
2·6	·0047	·0045	·0044	·0043	·0041	·0040	·0039	·0038	·0037	·0036
2·7	·0035	·0034	·0033	·0032	·0031	·0030	·0029	·0028	·0027	·0026
2·8	·0026	·0025	·0024	·0023	·0023	·0022	·0021	·0021	·0020	·0019
2·9	·0019	·0018	·0018	·0017	·0016	·0016	·0015	·0015	·0014	·0014
3·0	·0013	·0013	·0013	·0012	·0012	·0011	·0011	·0010	·0010	·0010
3·1	·0010	·0009	·0009	·0009	·0008	·0008	·0008	·0008	·0007	·0007
3·2	·0007									
3·3	·0005									
3·4	·0003									
3·5	·00023									
3·6	·00016									
3·7	·00011									
3·8	·00007									
3·9	·00005									
4·0	·00003									

Table II The *t* distribution

Critical values of *t* for a *two-tailed* test*

	Level of significance		
df	·10	·05	·02
1	6·314	12·706	31·821
2	2·920	4·303	6·965
3	2·353	3·182	4·541
4	2·132	2·776	3·747
5	2·015	2·571	3·365
6	1·943	2·447	3·143
7	1·895	2·365	2·998
8	1·860	2·306	2·896
9	1·833	2·262	2·821
10	1·812	2·228	2·764
11	1·796	2·201	2·718
12	1·782	2·179	2·681
13	1·771	2·160	2·650
14	1·761	2·145	2·624
15	1·753	2·131	2·602
16	1·746	2·120	2·583
17	1·740	2·110	2·567
18	1·734	2·101	2·552
19	1·729	2·093	2·539
20	2·086	2·086	2·528
21	1·721	2·080	2·518
22	1·717	2·074	2·508
23	1·714	2·069	2·500
24	1·711	2·064	2·492
25	1·708	2·060	2·485
26	1·706	2·056	2·479
27	1·703	2·052	2·473
28	1·701	2·048	2·467
29	1·699	2·045	2·462
30	1·697	2·042	2·457
40	1·684	2·021	2·423
60	1·671	2·000	2·390
120	1·658	1·980	2·358
∞	1·645	1·960	2·326

*For a *one-tailed* test the significance levels should be divided by 2.

Abridged from Table III of Fisher, F. A. and Yates, F. (1974) *Statistical Tables for Biological, Agricultural and Medical Research* 6th edn, London, Longman (previously published by Oliver & Boyd, Edinburgh) by permission of the authors and publisher.

Table III Chi-square

Critical values of chi-square (for one degree of freedom the significance levels are *two-tailed*, see p. 96)

	Level of significance				*Level of significance*		
df	·10	·05	·01	*df*	·10	·05	·01
1	2·71	3·84	6·64	16	23·54	26·30	32·00
2	4·60	5·99	9·21	17	24·77	27·59	33·41
3	6·25	7·82	11·34	18	25·99	28·87	34·80
4	7·78	9·49	13·28	19	27·20	30·14	36·19
5	9·24	11·07	15·09	20	28·41	31·41	37·57
6	10·64	12·59	16·81	21	29·62	32·67	38·93
7	12·02	14·07	18·48	22	30·81	33·92	40·29
8	13·36	15·51	20·09	23	32·01	35·17	41·64
9	14·68	16·92	21·67	24	33·20	36·42	42·98
10	15·99	18·31	23·21	25	34·38	37·65	44·31
11	17·28	19·68	24·72	26	35·56	38·88	45·64
12	18·55	21·03	26·22	27	36·74	40·11	46·96
13	19·81	22·36	27·69	28	37·92	41·34	48·28
14	21·06	23·68	29·14	29	39·09	42·56	49·59
15	22·31	25·00	30·58	30	40·26	43·77	50·89

Abridged from Table IV of Fisher and Yates (op. cit.), by permission of the authors and publisher.

Table IV Sign test

Critical values of *x* (the number of cases with the *less* frequent sign) for a *one-tailed* test* *N* is the total number of cases.

N	·05	·025	·01	N	·05	·025	·01
	Level of significance				*Level of significance*		
5	0	—	—	16	4	3	2
6	0	0	—	17	4	4	3
7	0	0	0	18	5	4	3
8	1	0	0	19	5	4	4
9	1	1	0	20	5	5	4
10	1	1	0				
				21	6	5	4
11	2	1	1	22	6	5	5
12	2	2	1	23	7	6	5
13	3	2	1	24	7	6	5
14	3	2	2	25	7	7	6
15	3	3	2				

*For a *two-tailed* test the significance levels should be multiplied by 2.

Table V Wilcoxon test

Critical values of *T* for a *two-tailed* test*

N	·05	·02	·01	N	·05	·02	·01
	Level of significance				*Level of significance*		
6	0	—	—	16	30	24	20
7	2	0	—	17	35	28	23
8	4	2	0	18	40	33	28
9	6	3	2	19	46	38	32
10	8	5	3	20	52	43	38
11	11	7	5	21	59	49	43
12	14	10	7	22	66	56	49
13	17	13	10	23	73	62	55
14	21	16	13	24	81	69	61
15	25	20	16	25	89	77	68

*For a *one-tailed* test the significance levels should be divided by 2.
Adapted from Table I of Wilcoxon, F. (1949) *Some Rapid Approximate Statistical Procedures*, New York, American Cyanamid Company, by permission of the publisher.

Table VI Mann-Whitney test

Critical values of U for a *two-tailed* test at 5 per cent significance*

N_2 \ N_1	5	6	7	8	9	10	11	12	13	14	15	16	17	18	19	20
5	2	3	5	6	7	8	9	11	12	13	14	15	17	18	19	20
6		5	6	8	10	11	13	14	16	17	19	21	22	24	25	27
7			8	10	12	14	16	18	20	22	24	26	28	30	32	34
8				13	15	17	19	22	24	26	29	31	34	36	38	41
9					17	20	23	26	28	31	34	37	39	42	45	48
10						23	26	29	33	36	39	42	45	48	52	55
11							30	33	37	40	44	47	51	55	58	62
12								37	41	45	49	53	57	61	65	69
13									45	50	54	59	63	67	72	76
14										55	59	64	67	74	78	83
15											64	70	75	80	85	90
16												75	81	86	92	98
17													87	93	99	105
18														99	106	112
19															113	119
20																127

*For a *one-tailed* test the values are significant at the 2½ per cent level.

Table VII Critical values of Spearman's r_s

Critical values of r_s for a *two-tailed* test*

	Level of significance			*Level of significance*			*Level of significance*	
N	·05	·01	*N*	·05	·01	*N*	·05	·01
5	1·00	—	14	·54	·69	23	·42	·54
6	·89	1·00	15	·52	·66	24	·41	·53
7	·79	·93	16	·51	·64	25	·40	·52
8	·74	·88	17	·49	·62	26	·39	·51
9	·68	·83	18	·48	·61	27	·38	·50
10	·65	·79	19	·46	·60	28	·38	·49
11	·61	·77	20	·45	·58	29	·37	·48
12	·59	·75	21	·44	·56	30	·36	·47
13	·56	·71	22	·43	·55			

*For a *one-tailed* test significance levels should be divided by 2.

Table VIII The F-test: Critical values of F at 5 per cent significance (*one-tailed*)*

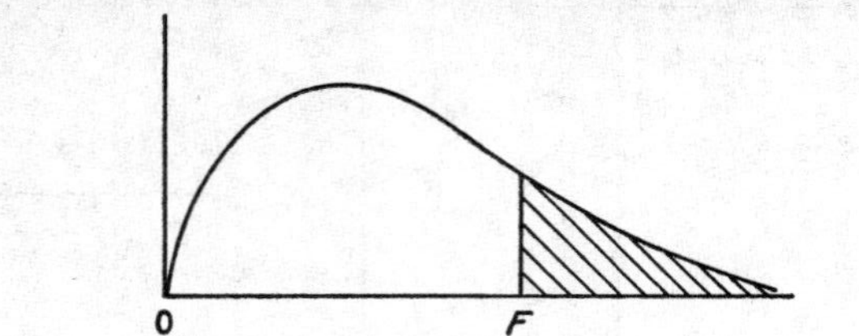

df in denominator	*Degrees of freedom in numerator*														
	1	*2*	*3*	*4*	*5*	*6*	*7*	*8*	*9*	*10*	*15*	*20*	*30*	*60*	*120*
1	161·40	199·50	215·70	224·60	230·30	234·00	236·80	238·90	240·50	241·90	245·90	248·00	250·10	252·20	253·30
2	18·51	19·00	19·16	19·25	19·30	19·33	19·35	19·35	19·38	19·43	19·43	19·45	19·46	19·48	19·49
3	10·13	9·55	9·28	9·12	9·01	8·94	8·89	8·85	8·81	8·79	8·70	8·66	8·62	8·57	8·55
4	7·71	6·94	6·59	6·39	6·26	6·16	6·09	6·04	6·00	5·96	5·86	5·80	5·75	5·69	5·66
5	6·61	5·79	5·41	5·19	5·05	4·95	4·88	4·82	4·77	4·74	4·62	4·56	4·50	4·43	4·40
6	5·99	5·14	4·76	4·53	4·39	4·28	4·21	4·15	4·10	4·06	3·94	3·87	3·81	3·74	3·70

7	5·59	4·74	4·35	4·12	3·97	3·87	3·79	3·73	3·68	3·64	3·51	3·44	3·38	3·30	3·27
8	5·32	4·46	4·07	3·84	3·69	3·58	3·50	3·44	3·39	3·35	3·22	3·15	3·08	3·01	2·97
9	5·12	4·26	3·86	3·63	3·48	3·37	3·29	3·23	3·18	3·14	3·01	2·94	2·86	2·79	2·75
10	4·96	4·10	3·71	3·48	3·33	3·22	3·14	3·07	3·02	2·98	2·85	2·77	2·70	2·62	2·58
11	4·84	3·98	3·59	3·36	3·20	3·09	3·01	2·95	2·90	2·85	2·72	2·65	2·57	2·49	2·45
12	4·75	3·89	3·49	3·26	3·11	3·00	2·91	2·85	2·80	2·75	2·62	2·54	2·47	2·38	2·34
13	4·67	3·81	3·41	3·18	3·03	2·92	2·83	2·77	2·71	2·67	2·53	2·46	2·38	2·30	2·25
14	4·60	3·74	3·34	3·11	2·96	2·85	2·76	2·70	2·65	2·60	2·46	2·39	2·31	2·22	2·18
15	4·54	3·68	3·29	3·06	2·90	2·79	2·71	2·64	2·59	2·54	2·40	2·33	2·25	2·16	2·11
16	4·49	3·63	3·24	3·01	2·85	2·74	2·66	2·59	2·54	2·49	2·35	2·28	2·19	2·11	2·06
17	4·45	3·59	3·20	2·96	2·81	2·70	2·61	2·55	2·49	2·45	2·31	2·23	2·15	2·06	2·01
18	4·41	3·55	3·16	2·93	2·77	2·66	2·58	2·51	2·46	2·41	2·27	2·19	2·11	2·02	1·97
19	4·38	3·52	3·13	2·90	2·74	2·63	2·54	2·48	2·42	2·38	2·23	2·16	2·07	1·98	1·93
20	4·35	3·49	3·10	2·87	2·71	2·60	2·51	2·45	2·39	2·35	2·20	2·12	2·04	1·95	1·90
25	4·24	3·39	2·99	2·76	2·60	2·49	2·40	2·34	2·28	2·24	2·09	2·01	1·92	1·82	1·77
30	4·17	3·32	2·92	2·69	2·53	2·42	2·33	2·27	2·21	2·16	2·10	1·93	1·84	1·74	1·68
40	4·08	3·23	2·84	2·61	2·45	2·34	2·25	2·18	2·12	2·08	1·92	1·84	1·74	1·64	1·58
60	4·00	3·15	2·76	2·53	2·37	2·25	2·17	2·10	2·04	1·99	1·84	1·75	1·65	1·53	1·47
120	3·92	3·07	2·68	2·45	2·29	2·17	2·09	2·02	1·95	1·91	1·75	1·66	1·55	1·43	1·35

*If the larger variance was not predicted (i.e. test is *two-tailed*) the significance level is 10 per cent.
From Merrington, M. and Thompson, C. M. (1943) 'Tables of percentage of the inverted beta (F) distribution', *Biometrika (33)*, 73–88.

Table IX Jonckheere trend test: minimum values of S (*one-tailed*)*

Significance level 0·05

No. of samples	*No. per sample* 2	3	4	5	6	7	8	9	10
3	10	17	24	33	42	53	64	76	88
4	14	26	38	51	66	82	100	118	138
5	20	34	51	71	92	115	140	166	194
6	26	44	67	93	121	151	184	219	256

Significance level 0·01

No. of samples	*No. per sample* 2	3	4	5	6	7	8	9	10
3	—	23	32	45	59	74	90	106	124
4	20	34	50	71	92	115	140	167	195
5	26	48	72	99	129	162	197	234	274
6	34	62	94	130	170	213	260	309	361

*For a *two-tailed* test (where direction of trend is not predicted) significance levels should be doubled.
From Jonckheere, A. R. (1954) *Biometrika (41)*, 133–5.

Table X Table of critical values of L

	·05 *Level of significance* k						·01 *Level of significance* k					
N	3	4	5	6	7	8	3	4	5	6	7	8
2	28	58	103	166	252	362	—	60	106	173	261	376
3	41	84	150	244	370	532	42	87	155	252	382	549
4	54	111	197	321	487	701	55	114	204	331	501	722
5	66	137	244	397	603	869	68	141	251	409	620	893
6	79	163	291	474	719	1037	81	167	299	486	737	1063
7	91	189	338	550	835	1204	93	193	346	563	855	1232
8	104	214	384	625	950	1371	106	220	393	640	972	1401
9	116	240	431	701	1065	1537	119	246	441	717	1088	1569
10	128	266	477	777	1180	1703	131	272	487	793	1205	1736
11	141	292	523	852	1295	1868	144	298	534	869	1321	1905
12	153	317	570	928	1410	2035	156	324	581	946	1437	2072
	4·25	6·60	9·50	12·9	16·8	21·2	4·34	6·75	9·68	13·1	17·0	21·6

For $N > 12$, the value of L is significant if L/kN exceeds the value in the last row of the table.
From Page, E. E. (1963), *J. Amer. Statist. Assoc. (58)*, 216–30.

Table XI Critical values of the product–moment correlation coefficient*

The size of the sample is given in the left-hand column. An obtained correlation coefficient must be as large as or larger than the value in the body of the table to be significant at the level of significance stated for the column.

	Level of significance for two-tailed test			
N	·10	·05	·02	·01
3	·988	·997	·9995	·9999
4	·900	·950	·980	·990
5	·805	·878	·934	·959
6	·729	·811	·882	·917
7	·669	·754	·833	·874
8	·622	·707	·789	·834
9	·582	·666	·750	·798
10	·549	·632	·716	·765
11	·521	·602	·685	·735
12	·497	·576	·658	·708
13	·476	·553	·634	·684
14	·458	·532	·612	·661
15	·441	·514	·592	·641
16	·426	·497	·574	·623
17	·412	·482	·558	·606
18	·400	·468	·542	·590
19	·389	·456	·528	·575
20	·378	·444	·516	·561
21	·369	·433	·503	·549
22	·360	·423	·492	·537
23	·352	·413	·482	·526
24	·344	·404	·472	·515
25	·337	·396	·462	·505
26	·330	·388	·453	·496
27	·323	·381	·445	·487
28	·317	·374	·437	·479
29	·311	·367	·430	·471
30	·306	·361	·423	·463

*Abridged from Fisher and Yates (op. cit.), by permission of the authors and publisher.

References and name index

(The numbers in italics following each reference refer to page numbers within this book.)

Blalock, H. M. (1972) *Social Statistics*, New York, McGraw-Hill. *28*

Boneau, C. A. (1960) 'The effects of violations of assumptions underlying the *t*-test', *Psychological Bulletin*, 57, 49–64. *65*

Chambers, R. G. (1982) 'Correlation coefficients from 2 × 2 tables and from biserial data', *British Journal of Mathematical and Statistical Psychology*, 35, 2. *97*

Chatfield, C. and Collins, A. J. (1980) *Introduction to Multivariate Analysis*, London, Chapman & Hall. *7*

Edgington, E. S. (1969) *Statistical Inference*, New York, McGraw-Hill. *93, 161*

Gardiner, J. M. and Kaminska, Z. (1975) *First Experiments in Psychology*, London, Methuen. *152*

Goodman, R. (1962) *Teach Yourself Statistics*, London, English Universities Press. *74*

Jonkheere, A. R. (1954) *Biometrika*, 41, 133–5. *126*

Kolstoe, R. H. (1973) *Introduction to Statistics for the Behavioral Sciences*, Illinois, Dorsey Press. *51, 108*

Meddis, R. (1973) *Elementary Analysis of Variance for the Behavioural Sciences*, Maidenhead, McGraw-Hill. *126*

Miller, S. H. (forthcoming) *Multivariate Design and Statistics*, London, Methuen. 7, *151*
Myers, J. L. (1962) *Fundamentals of Experimental Design*, Boston, Allyn & Bacon. *14*
Page, E. E. (1963) *Journal of American Statistical Association*, 58, 216–30. *126*
Poulton, E. C. (1980) 'Range effects and asymmetric transfer in studies of motor skill', in Nadeau, C. H., *et al.* (eds) *Psychology of Motor Behavior and Sport*, Champaign, Illinois, Human Kinetics Pub. Inc. *12*
Siegel, S. (1956) *Non-parametric Statistics for the Behavioral Sciences*, New York, McGraw-Hill. *88, 93, 142*
Singer, B. (1979) *Distribution-Free Methods for Non-parametric Problems: A Classified and Selected Bibliography*, Leicester, British Psychological Society. *64*
Stone, L. A. and James, R. (1965) 'Interval scaling of the prestige of selected secondary education teacher-specialists', *Perceptual and Motor Skills*, 20, 859–60. *63*
Wallis, W. A. and Roberts, H. V. (1963) *Statistics: A New Approach*, New York, Free Press. *28*

Subject index